Mary

in the Plan of God and in the Communion of Saints

MARY IN THE PLAN OF GOD AND IN THE COMMUNION OF SAINTS

Toward a Common Christian Understanding

BY
ALAIN BLANCY AND MAURICE JOURJON
AND THE DOMBES GROUP

Translated by Matthew J. O'Connell

Foreword by Joseph A. Fitzmyer, S.J.

PAULIST PRESS
New York/Mahwah, N.J.

Cover design by Valerie Petro

Cover image is from a mosaic at the National Shrine of Our Lady of the Snows, Belleville, Ill.

Book design by Theresa M. Sparacio

Library of Congress Cataloging-in-Publication Data

Blancy, Alain.
[Marie dans le dessein de Dieu et la communion des saints. English]
Mary in the plan of God and in the communion of saints : toward a common Christian understanding / by Alain Blancy and Maurice Jourjon and the Dombes Group ; foreword by Joseph A. Fitzmyer ; translated by Matthew J. O'Connell.
p. cm.
Includes bibliographical references and index.
ISBN 0-8091-4069-1 (alk. paper)
1. Mary, Blessed Virgin, Saint—Theology. 2. Mary, Blessed Virgin, Saint, and Christian union. 3. Catholic Church—Relations—Protestant churches. 4. Protestant churches—Relations—Catholic Church. I. Title.

BT613 .B5613 2002
232.91—dc21

2002020726

Published by Paulist Press
997 Macarthur Boulevard
Mahwah, New Jersey 07430

www.paulistpress.com

Printed and bound in the
United States of America

Contents

My soul magnifies the Lord
and my spirit rejoices in God my Savior,
for he has looked with favor on the lowliness of his servant.
Surely, from now on all generations will call me blessed;
for the Mighty One has done great things for me,
and holy is his name.
His mercy is for those who fear him
from generation to generation.
He has shown strength with his arm;
he has scattered the proud in the thoughts of their hearts.
He has brought down the powerful from their thrones,
and lifted up the lowly;
he has filled the hungry with good things,
and sent the rich away empty.
He has helped his servant Israel,
in remembrance of his mercy,
according to the promise he made to our ancestors,
to Abraham and to his descendants forever.
(Luke 1:46–55 NRSV)

Foreword

Christianity in the twentieth century was marked by an ecumenical movement about which preceding centuries knew almost nothing. Christianity then became in a new sense a worldwide religion and began to seek a unity that had been damaged by divisions in the eleventh and sixteenth centuries.

At the beginning of the twentieth century, the ecumenical movement was largely the endeavor of Protestant Christians, both of the reformed and free church traditions, who sought to evangelize the world of that generation. After the First World War, Orthodox Christians joined them and contributed much to the movement, especially when the Ecumenical Patriarchate proposed the formation of a league of churches, which led in time to the establishment of the World Council of Churches (1948). After the Second World War, Roman Catholics began to grope tentatively toward such Christian unity, but it was not until the Second Vatican Council (1962–1965) that ecumenism became a major concern. Once the Council had issued its principles of ecumenism and recognized that other Christians, through faith and baptism, have been "brought into a certain, though imperfect, communion with the Catholic Church" (*Unitatis redintegratio* 3), many serious moves and bilateral consultations on national and international levels were undertaken in the late 1960s and have continued until the present day. These were aimed at overcoming the historic divisions among Christians inherited from previous centuries. Noteworthy among such consultations was the signing of the *Joint Declaration on the Doctrine of Justification* by official representatives of the

Catholic Church and the Lutheran World Federation in Augsburg on October 31, 1999.

As early as 1937, however, French-speaking ecumenists had gathered in France to address the question of Christian unity, and they are known today as *Le Groupe des Dombes*. This group grew out of the efforts of Abbé Paul Couturier (d. 1953), a priest of the archdiocese of Lyons in France. He brought together several Protestant pastors and Catholic priests from France and Switzerland, who were interested in promoting Christian unity, to a dialogue that was held often at the Cistercian abbey of Notre Dame des Dombes, situated about 20 miles north of Lyons, whence came the name for the group. Today Le Groupe des Dombes still meets once a year in early September and is made up of twenty Catholic and twenty Lutheran or Reformed theologians. Since 1997, they have been meeting at the Benedictine abbey of Pradines, near Roanne in the Loire Valley.

This French-speaking ecumenical group is a private association, sponsored officially by no church, but the secretaries of the ecumenical division of the Fédération Protestante de France and of the French Episcopal Conference usually are among the twenty on each side. Moreover, Anglican and Orthodox theologians are invited regularly to attend the sessions. All of the members share a common theological interest and are concerned with studying and praying together in order to overcome the historic divisions that have plagued the Christian Church, especially since the sixteenth century. Their goal is to clear the way for the union of Christian Churches by gradually removing the obstacles to that union inherited from previous centuries and to formulate anew the common Christian faith. Part of that goal is also a call for *metanoia*, a change of heart and mind, and for *conversio*, a willingness to recognize the faults and errors on both sides that have caused the division and to push for a really mutual conversion. Their meetings are marked by periods of meditation, study, and prayer together; each day the liturgy is celebrated, Catholic or Protestant. The co-presidents of the Groupe recently have been Pasteur Alain Blancy of Farges and Père Maurice Jourjon of Lyons.

For almost two decades the Groupe des Dombes studied privately a variety of theological topics such as justification, redemption, the sacraments, and the church, usually in a confrontational mode. As of

1956, the Groupe began to speak out publicly on ecclesiological topics, now in a more collaborative mode. From 1956 to 1970 it published a series of "theses," and from 1971 to 1998 another series, called "documents." Some of the topics treated between 1956 and 1970 were the following: "The Mediation of Christ and the Ministry of the Church" (1957); "The Church as the Body of Christ" (1958); "The Pastoral Authority of the Church" (1959); "The Apostolicity of the Church" (1960): "The Priesthood and the Ministry of the Church" (1961); "Christ's Priestly Act in the Priestly Activity of the Church" (1962); "The Church and the Holy Spirit" (1969); "The Church as the Communion of Saints" (1970).

As of 1971, the published documents have taken on a wider scope and have stressed the points on which the Christian churches find ecumenical agreement. Five booklets have been devoted to such topics as "Toward One Eucharistic Faith?" (1971); "For a reconciliation of Ministries" (1972); "The Ministry of the Bishop" (1976); "The Holy Spirit, the Church, and the Sacraments" (1979); "The Ministry of Communion in the Universal Church" (1985).

To mark the fiftieth anniversary of the Groupe des Dombes in 1987, the earlier theses and documents were collected in one volume and published under the title, *Pour la communion des Églises: L'Apport du Groupe des Dombes (1937–1987)* (Paris: Le Centurion, 1988). A second volume appeared in 1991, entitled *Pour la conversion des Églises: Identité et changement dans la dynamique de la communion* (Paris: Le Centurion).

In order to test the degree to which the two sides were committed to such a conversion of Churches, the Groupe devoted its annual sessions from 1991 to 1997 to reflection and discussion of Mary's role in God's plan of salvation. The result of that consultation appeared in two booklets: *Marie dans le dessein de Dieu et la communion des saints: I. Dans l'histoire et l'Écriture* (Paris: Bayard Editions/Le Centurion, 1997) and *II. Controverse et conversion* (1998). A second edition united the two booklets under the simple title *Marie: Dans le dessein de Dieu et la communion des saints* (Paris: Bayard Editions/Le Centurion, 1999). The book thus treats questions often debated between Catholics and Protestants: Mary's cooperation in the salvation offered by Christ; the dogmas of the Immaculate Conception and Assumption; the virginity of Mary; and prayer addressed to Mary.

The treatment of these topics also included an appeal to Christians on both sides to purify and modify the excess of their language about Mary and to remedy the deficit of expression in order to situate Mary, the Mother of God *(Theotokos)*, in her rightful place in God's salvific plan and in the communion of saints.

This publication of 1999 is now being presented here in English translation, *Mary in the Plan of God and in the Communion of Saints*, and it introduces the English-speaking world to the significant work of the Groupe des Dombes on this very sensitive issue among modern Christians. The reader will note the book's two parts, reflecting the original booklets, as well as its two prefaces written by the co-presidents of the Groupe des Dombes, Pastor Alain Blancy and Father Maurice Jourjon. The prefaces are a good introduction to the reading of the document as a whole; they also familiarize the reader with the circumstances in which the document took shape and with the concerns that guided its lengthy discussion and composition.

English-speaking readers will recall that in 1978 twelve American New Testament scholars published the results of a common study of the biblical passages mentioning Mary, the Mother of the Lord. It was entitled *Mary in the New Testament: A Collaborative Assessment by Protestant and Roman Catholic Scholars* (ed. R. E. Brown et al., New York: Paulist Press; Philadelphia: Fortress). Of the twelve who contributed to the discussion four were Catholic, four were Lutheran, and four were non-Lutheran Protestants, which represented an attempt to have contributions to the collaborative study from several Christian bodies. That study had been sponsored by the USA national dialogue of Lutherans and Roman Catholics and eventually contributed to the dialogue's discussion of *The One Mediator, the Saints, and Mary* (Lutherans and Catholics in Dialogue 8, ed. H. G. Anderson et al., Minneapolis, Minn.: Augsburg, 1992). Whereas the American book, *Mary in the New Testament*, was devoted only to the biblical data on Mary, the present book of the Groupe des Dombes, while not neglecting the New Testament material, discusses the larger theological issues about the role of the Blessed Mother in God's plan of salvation in the living dogmatic tradition of the church as a whole.

This book, then, is a remarkable study of the issues that Catholics and Protestants have always raised with each other about

Mary. It not only presents an ecumenical reading of the data from scripture and history, but also discusses sanely the Marian questions disputed by Catholics and Protestants. Moreover, it lays out a wise plan for the conversion of the churches, showing how Protestants and Catholics can eventually become a reunited Christian Church despite differences about Mary—for such differences are seen as not necessarily church-dividing.

Joseph A. Fitzmyer, S.J.

PART I

An Ecumenical Reading of History and Scripture

Preface for Part I

Editorial Note

The original French publication of this work was accomplished in two stages: Part I appeared in January 1997 and Part II twelve months later. The English edition is retaining the original Preface for Part I even though, in this edition, the two parts have been joined in a single volume.

In a departure from its usual procedure, the Dombes Group is publishing separately the first part of a document titled *Mary in the Plan of God and in the Communion of Saints*; the second half will appear as soon as possible. There are several reasons for this publication in two stages.

First of all, the subject is a relatively new one in ecumenical discussion. It does not yet figure in the agenda of any of the present major worldwide interconfessional dialogues. This situation forced the Group to proceed more slowly and to develop at greater length some aspects of the subject. For this reason, the work has not yet been fully completed. On the other hand, the first part seems sufficiently developed for immediate publication. The Group thinks that, in response to legitimate expectations, it owes it to its readers and to the members of our churches to make known at more or less regular intervals the progress it is making.

A second and better reason is that this part can stand on its own because it begins with information and then gives a rereading of the biblical texts in the framework of the confessions of faith. It thereby prepares the way for the part that will deal with continuing disagreements. It is thus not a simple announcement, much less a preface, to the second part. It constitutes a whole. To use an expression of Irenaeus, we are really talking of Mary's place in the symphony of salvation, and this symphony is not unfinished.

In deciding on the publication of this first part, the Group is also sharing with its readers its own itinerary. In fidelity to its ecumenical principle,[1] it has attempted in this first part to engage in a joint reading of history and scripture, while also keeping in mind the need to examine and even surmount remaining disagreements and to suggest to the Christians and churches concerned some concrete steps toward conversion.

If the Dombes Group advances at its own pace, each dossier leading to the next, it desires no less strongly to listen to its own times and give answers to the urgent questions that emerge there. In the Group's view, such an urgent question has presently arisen due to a disordered revival of ill-informed Marian piety that is only aggravating the tensions already existing between the churches in regard to the place of Mary, or even tensions arising within one and the same church. The Group realizes that many of these attitudes come from an ignorance of history and from a controverted reading of scripture, and it thinks it opportune not to wait for the completion of its work before contributing to a clarification of these matters.

The title of the document signals two issues that intersect like vertical and horizontal axes. *Mary in the Plan of God* seeks to define the place that the Virgin has in the mysterious work of salvation by reason of her closeness to the Son of God who was to become her own child. *Mary in the Communion of Saints* seeks to understand her place in the church of heaven and earth and in the company of the saints of every place and time, namely, the faithful: the mother of God is the sister of believers. One and the same salvation is at work in the mystery of the incarnation and in universal redemption. Mary, placed as she is where these two movements intersect, is both witness to them and manifestation of them. In its second part, the document will explore the conditions for and the consequences of the intersection of these two axes.

It is only together that we were able to write the history of our faith, and it is together that we have searched this history in order to draw lessons from it.

If our reflections take up more room than reflections in earlier documents, it is not because the subject is more central to the faith. We need to remind ourselves forcefully that Mary has never been a cause of separation among the churches. On the contrary, she has become a victim and even a virulent expression of such separations. A number of other factors of disunity are polarized around her and made visible in her. This is why the Group has decided to deal with this individual who is emblematic of the Christian faith and tradition, if for no other reason than to justify, in a concrete and decidedly sensitive issue, its own working method and the call for ecclesial conversion that runs through all of its texts. Is it possible to speak a common language and promote a mutual change of heart on a sensitive matter that brings into play the sensibilities and piety of both sides? Any move toward reconciliation here will have repercussions in other areas.

Our Group is at one in saying that the plan of God, as revealed by the Bible and received by the faith that "regulates" *(regula fidei)* and "expresses itself" in confessions of faith according to the three articles of the Creed, links together virginal conception and motherhood: he who died under Pontius Pilate was born of the Virgin Mary.

The faith of the undivided church, which exists today in each person among us, gives the church its unity and makes the communion of saints a reality in its mysterious wholeness: The salvation wrought by Christ is a work not of human persuasion but of God's power. Lo! the barren woman gives birth and the Virgin conceives, and in this event the poor are already being evangelized. At the dawn of the third millennium, is there anywhere a confession of faith in Christ the Savior that would reject this fidelity to the gospel?

Mary in the confessions of faith does not differ from Mary in scripture. The Infancy Gospels are to the synoptics what the Prologue is to the Gospel of John, that is, less a history or prehistory of Jesus than a witness to the self-emptying of him who is to be raised on high and called Lord to the glory of God the Father (see Phil 2:6–11). Together, therefore, we listen to the message sent to Mary and to her Magnificat, for it is together that we confess Jesus to be "conceived by the Holy Spirit and born of the Virgin Mary."

The Group has done its work all the more serenely because it has been able to differentiate between what faith demands and what devotion allows. This basic distinction is at work throughout the document. Some authors of the Middle Ages could write: "We will never say enough about Mary!"; at the same time, however, it is no less important to distinguish between devotional freedom (within the limits set by the rule of faith) and the one thing necessary. Regarding this last, the Augsburg Confession (1530/1580) recalls the principle *Satis est* ("It is enough!"): that is, what suffices for the existence of the church and of church unity: "the correct preaching of the gospel and the faithful administration of the sacraments." The "hierarchy of truths" of which Vatican II speaks reflects to a large extent the same concern. As we shall see, the point of departure is the common confession of faith as seen in the creeds of the early church. Both the Apostles' Creed and the Nicene-Constantinopolitan Creed (381) expressly mention Mary and contrast her with Pilate—as birth to death, as participation in the mystery of the incarnation to complicity in the passion.

The positive character of the results reached at this stage is an encouraging sign for the step that will follow and that is indeed already being taken. As we shall see, the summary of the second volume (Part II of the present work) shows both the breadth and the sensitive nature of the area still to be covered. But it is already possible to bear witness to the state of mind that has animated the forty members of the Group during these five years of work. The joy experienced by pioneers has been the predominant feeling, despite or even because of the risk taken in committing ourselves to this work on a subject on which major interconfessional dialogues have not yet begun. The joy, too, of discovering that disagreement does not necessarily follow the hardened lines dividing the confessions. Christians can have personal feelings and attitudes of respect, even of veneration, for the mother of their Lord and Savior.

The list of participants in this work contains only men. This does not mean that the text has been worked up without female participation. Death has taken one partner from us: France Queré. But the question of female collaboration does not arise solely in connection with a subject involving a woman. It holds for any article of the faith. The method of co-opting members for a private group and the necessity of continuity in a work once begun only postpone for the time being the desired deadline for regular participation by women in and outside the Group.

The Group has always been able to do its work in an atmosphere of serenity that has not excluded either rigorous debate or the head-on clash of convictions. This has been possible due to a spirit of brotherhood created over the years and matched by a spiritual life that has been fed by the prayer of the monks of the abbey whose name the Group has borne for almost sixty years in a spirit of thanksgiving, humility, and responsibility.

It is therefore with confidence that we offer the present work to our readers, and we await responses which we shall be able to take into account later on in a fruitful dialogue with these same readers.

The readers will forgive us if, in the midst of our gratitude to God, we feel some pride that we have been able to work together on a subject that is divisive and still divides us. For while the Virgin Mary is a necessary note in the symphony of salvation, this note does not immediately create harmony among us. Yet the fact that we jointly admit this is anything but a confession of failure. It is rather an act of remembrance (anamnesis) that gives rise to repentance and hope. To acknowledge jointly what still divides us is, in a way, to speak to the past. By marking this first section of our work not with the word "end" but with the words "to be continued," we are saying to our respective churches: This is what divided us yesterday. What will be the case tomorrow, since the future provides the today of our faith?

Alain Blancy and Maurice Jourjon
Co-presidents of the Dombes Group

Introduction

1. After over fifty years of patient ecumenical work in the area of doctrine and after the appearance of its most recent document calling for the conversion of the churches, the Dombe Group believes that a further bold step is now possible: To tackle the subject of the Virgin Mary. In the traditions of our churches this subject is especially liable to cause conflict, both because of the stake the Christian faith has in it and because of the opposite affective reactions it continually elicits. We have therefore tried to propose a way of conversion, in the spirit of our preceding document, *Pour la conversion des Églises.*[1]

2. Enlightened by our earlier studies, we have decided to begin with historical testimonies and only later on offer a joint reading of what the scriptures say of Mary. It is important that we all be clear about the place of Mary in the tradition of the first millennium, a tradition we all accept, and then about the way in which she became a subject of growing disagreement during the Reformation period (Chapter 1).

3. We have endeavored, next, to bring out everything that unites us in a joint confession of faith in which Mary has the place belonging to her in the Christian economy of salvation. This is why we have chosen the three articles of the creed as the framework for presenting Mary as a creature of the Father, like all other creatures, as the mother of the Son who came to take flesh in our world, and as the woman who was present in the praying community of Pentecost and belongs, through the Spirit, to the community of saints which is the church. It is in this framework that we shall read once more the testimonies of the scriptures about Mary (Chapter 2).

4. At that point we shall go on to tackle the four main points of disagreement among us: Did Mary "cooperate" in our salvation, or did she not? Did she remain perpetually a virgin, or did she have other children, the brothers and sisters of Jesus? What of the dogmas defined on the Catholic side: the Immaculate Conception and the Assumption? Finally, is it legitimate to call on Mary in prayer and ask her to intercede with God (Chapter 3)?

5. Finally, we shall suggest to our churches some steps in a confessional conversion, in the hope that Mary will no longer be a stumbling block between us (Chapter 4).

6. Our readings of history, of the scriptural witness, and of our agreements and remaining disagreements will obviously be made in an ecumenical spirit and in an ecclesiological setting. The perspective of a call to conversion will be present in each of our chapters. This does not mean any intention of denying all our differences; rather, it indicates a desire to understand these differences according to what they really mean and to respect the sensitivities of both sides.

7. We are aware that since we are among the first to engage in a thorough interconfessional dialogue on the subject of Mary, our work can only be a clearing of the ground. Our aim is to inspire other works and take part in an advance of our churches toward a peaceful attitude. The existing situation has forced us into longer and more technical explanations than we would have liked, but these seemed necessary for an accurate grasp of the subject—for it is really too bad that a major disagreement should have arisen among Christians about the mother of their Savior.

1

The Lessons of History

MARY IN THE EARLY CHURCH

8. ◆ Our study of the place of Mary in the early church covers, for practical purposes, the first millennium: it will focus, first, on the confessions of faith, then on the main writings of the Fathers of the Church, and finally on a very special literature, the New Testament "apocrypha," which played a role, to some extent, in the development of Marian devotion and in the liturgy and worship.

Mary in the Confession of Faith

9. In the earliest documents as well as in the most solemn, Mary is much less present than she is in the gospels. She has no place in the preaching of the apostles (*kerygma,* see Acts 2:14–36, etc.), she is missing from the earliest confessions of faith; and she is not at the heart of the first ecumenical councils. What is going on here?

10. The creeds, or symbols of the faith, went through a slow development until the beginning of the third century when we come upon the first creeds of the church. Well before that, however, we see the various elements of the future creeds being organized and structured in formulas created by writers. Ignatius of Antioch (ca. 110) is the first witness and gives us several christological sequences, all of them coming directly from the apostolic kerygma. In his formulas, references to the paschal mystery are preceded by references to the "true" (real, genuine) birth of Jesus: "In accordance with the divine plan, our God, Jesus Christ, was carried in the womb of Mary, being

born of the blood of David and also of the Holy Spirit."[1] Thus the mention of the virginal conception of Jesus as son of Mary entered into the confessions of faith at the very beginning of the second century; it would never henceforth be absent from them.

11. Irenaeus is the first Father of the Church to suggest explicitly (ca. 180) that Mary had a place in the preaching of the apostles. His account of the apostolic kerygma contains the following lines about Eve and Mary: "It was necessary...that a virgin, by becoming the advocate of a virgin, should destroy the disobedience of a virgin by the obedience of a virgin."[2]

12. The authority and reasonableness of Irenaeus, his reliance on the tradition of the churches of Asia Minor and especially on Polycarp, and the presence of the Mary-Eve comparison at two points in his great work *Against the Heresies*–all these encourage us to trust him when he locates Mary in the plan of salvation and justifies this by describing the preaching of the apostles. In the eyes of the bishop of Lyons, the explanation of faith in Christ calls for mention of the virginal conception, and scripture itself at its very beginning attests to the recapitulation of Adam in Christ via a movement of life from Mary to Eve. Such is the apostolic faith which the church "proclaims, teaches, and passes on."[3]

13. No creed repeats Irenaeus' views. But the Creed of Constantinople (which we call the Nicene-Constantinopolitan Creed) in 381 contains the name of Mary, as the Apostles' Creed already did (this creed originated in the baptismal creed attested in *The Apostolic Tradition* at the beginning of the third century):

> *Apostles' Creed:* "I believe...and in Jesus Christ, his only Son, our Lord, who was conceived by the power of the Holy Spirit and born of the Virgin Mary."
> *Nicene-Constantinopolitan Creed:* "I believe in one Lord, Jesus Christ....For us men and for our salvation he came down from heaven: by the power of the Holy Spirit he was born of the Virgin Mary, and became man."

In both creeds Mary is linked, as it were, to Pontius Pilate, and this catches our attention. Mary recalls the birth, Pilate recalls the death, and the two thus give Christ his historical dates.

14. But Mary's witness is of an entirely different order from Pilate's. The Roman official is a witness who has civil status. Mary bears witness to the unimpeachable conviction of a mother: she knows. Pilate is in no sense a witness, even an unwilling one, to the resurrection. The mystery of faith is completely beyond his ken. He is as it were external to the text that cites him. By reason of her virginity Mary witnesses to the mystery of the incarnation. There is here an expression of the faith. In neither of the two creeds is Mary present as a kind of ornament, as if she were simply part of the decor. If the apostolic faith focuses on the death and resurrection of the Lord, the concomitant implication is that the same faith has reached a decision on the birth of the same Lord in the light of his resurrection.

15. When we encounter Mary in the church of the seven ecumenical councils, the very mention of her is a profession of faith in Jesus the Lord; it is an open and correct expression of adoration of her Son. Faith in Jesus, Christ, Son of God, and Savior, whom Christians can receive like a fish in the palms of their hands, comes from the Virgin Mother Church.[4] But this faith is projected back, in a kind of cinematic dissolve, on the Virgin Mother Mary.

16. Historians automatically understand the words of the Council of Constantinople, "he was born of the Virgin Mary," to be an almost trite expression of the apostolic faith and based on the testimony of the gospels. If these historians take into account all seven of the seven councils, they will report that the Church of the Fathers, though divided on the subject of the specific dogma of Chalcedon and on the theology of images, shows no disagreement in its faith regarding the Virgin Mary, because this faith remains within the framework of biblical statements and statements about Christ.

17. In fact, there is, strictly speaking, no "Marian dogma" of Ephesus, and the mention of Mary has its place first of all not in the christological dogma of Chalcedon but in the creeds. In these creeds (Nicea, Constantinople, Apostles' Creed) we express our faith in Christ, the Word of God, who in order to save us took flesh of the Virgin Mary. As we shall see, the veneration of Mary that gradually developed had other sources besides the fundamental confession of faith, namely, that our Savior was born of the Virgin Mary, who,

through the obedience of faith, received into her womb the author of her own salvation.

Mary in Patristic Literature

18. The Marian theology of the early church is in fact a Christology, for the direct focus on Christ is what leads to speaking of the Virgin Mary as the Mother of Jesus, of the Christ and Savior who is God. We may say that this is the case from the beginning and especially from Irenaeus on (ca. 180) down to the Council of Ephesus (431). To call Mary the Mother of God *(Theotokos)* is indeed to speak of Christ.[5]

19. The virginal conception is one of the mysteries of salvation, since it is the sign of "God among us" (Emmanuel):

> *Irenaeus:* "There is only one selfsame Spirit of God who...proclaimed that the fullness of the time of adoptive sonship had come, that the kingdom of God was at hand, and that it dwelt within human beings who believed in Emmanuel born of the Virgin."[6]

This conception is also a sign of the birth of Christians from the "Virgin Mother Church":

> *Augustine* (d.430): "It was fitting that by a unique miracle our head was born physically from a virgin, thereby signifying that his members would be born spiritually from the virgin Church."[7]

It was for this reason that the postapostolic church, despite the reservations of some,[8] understood the virginal conception of Jesus as Mary's call to perpetual virginity:

> Origen: "According to those who think soundly of her, Mary had no other children besides Jesus."[9]

20. In the period after Ephesus the church gradually took the term *Theotokos* as a form of Marian praise:

> *5th Ecumenical Council, Constantinople II (533), can. 6:* "This is the pious sense in which the holy Council of Chalcedon confessed her to be the Mother of God."[10]

But it was Augustine who distinguished aspects of this divine motherhood that would be accepted later on[11]:

> "She is not spiritually the mother of our head, as that is the Savior himself. On the contrary, she was spiritually born from him....On the other hand, clearly she is the mother of his members, which is ourselves....She is physically the mother of the head himself."[12]

21. The existence in the church of consecrated female virginity has caused Mary, the model of virgins, to be looked upon as the first nun:

> *Athanasius (d. 373) to consecrated virgins:* "May the life of Mary, who gave birth to God, be for all of you the image in which each of you will live her virginity."[13]
> *Augustine:* "That motherhood of one holy virgin is an honor for all holy virgins."[14]

22. Mary's perfect holiness, understood as an absence of personal sins, is asserted by Augustine:

> "On account of the honor due to the Lord, I do not want to raise here any question about her when we are dealing with sins."[15]

Against Pelagius, Augustine asserts that it is by grace that Mary never sinned.[16] But the positions taken by some other Fathers show that the bishop of Hippo was not immediately followed in his views:

> *Cyril of Alexandria (d.444):* "By 'a sword' Simeon was referring to the keenness and violence of the sufferings that would lead Mary to express these inappropriate ideas, which reflected the bad side of her weak womanly spirit."[17]

23. On the other hand, Augustine's theology made unthinkable any assertion of Mary's immaculate conception: no one born of a fleshly union, which means everyone but Christ, is exempt from traces of original sin:

> *Augustine:* "He [who] was born of the Holy Spirit and the Virgin Mary [was] utterly free from any sin, because he was free from

> that conception which results from sexual union. Even Jeremiah and John, though they were made holy in the wombs of their mothers, still contracted original sin."[18]

24. Some Greek Fathers of the seventh and eighth centuries already seem to be thinking of the later, modern dogma:

> *Andrew of Crete, Bishop (d.740)*: "Mary, the first fruits, one in whom the entire corrupt mass of dough was not commingled."[19]

They also provide, in the person of John Damascene (d. ca. 749), an interesting statement about the dormition of Mary:

> "How could corruption take hold of this body that received Life within it? Nothing of that kind befits this soul and body that carried God within them."[20]

25. Any invocation of Mary, which was slow in coming (only the martyrs were invoked), certainly had popular and monastic origins:

> *The well-known prayer "Sub tuum"*: "We take refuge in the protection of your mercy, Mother of God *(Theotokos)*."[21]

26. Intensified as it was by Marian liturgical feasts, prayer to Mary gave rise in the East to lyrical outpourings that found few, if any, imitators among the Fathers of the Western Church. There is, for example, the well-known *Akathistos* hymn,[22] the date of which is uncertain, but which was perhaps the work of Romanus Melodus (d. ca. 555). Ambrose (d. 397), for his part, offers a fine example of western reserve in his meditation on Mary at the foot of the cross:

> "She was waiting not for the death of him who is our ransom, but for the salvation of the world. In addition, knowing that the redemption of the world was coming from the death of her Son, she perhaps thought that she had to add something to this gift....But Jesus had no need of help in saving all of us....He thus accepted the affection of a mother but did not look for help from anyone else."[23]

27. All in all, we might say that the church of the Fathers translated into prayer and veneration the Christological statements of Irenaeus about Mary, the obedient virgin and "cause of salvation":

> *Irenaeus:* "Mary, a virgin and obedient...became a cause of salvation for herself and for the entire human race....The knot of Eve's disobedience was untied by the obedience of Mary."[24] "She [Mary] was persuaded to obey God, in order that the virgin Mary might become the advocate of virgin Eve."[25]

28. The patristic texts we have been reading here may seem to go beyond the councils. In fact, however, these texts do not depend on the councils but, like the councils themselves, on scripture and the faith of the apostles. Then, too, the gap which we see between their belief and the letter of the scriptures (their assertion of Mary's perpetual virginity, for example) is seen by them not as a departure from the scriptures but as fruit of their conviction that the scriptures in their entirety are spiritual. This is why perpetual virginity, like the phrase "consubstantial with the Father," interprets the letter of the scriptures. That is how the Fathers, even those we describe as "literalists,"[26] read the scriptures.

29. Popular devotion sometimes anticipated doctrine when it came to praying to Mary. We note only that in the West popular piety has not found its way into the authentic prayer of the people of God, namely, liturgical worship, which alone is in question in the adage: "The law of prayer is the law of faith" *(Lex orandi, lex credendi)*. The Marian feasts are not invasive and remain unobtrusive, even if their origin is sometimes obscure.[27]

30. By way of conclusion to this first overview of the councils and the Fathers we can say that the basic reason for speaking of Mary, as the creeds and the Fathers do, springs from this twofold concern:

(1) In order to have a "correct" ("orthodox") faith in Christ, we must look at Mary in a way that does not turn us aside from her Son but, on the contrary, sees her as belonging to the contemplation of the very mysteries of Jesus.

(2) We must never say of Mary the slightest thing that would be inconsistent with the honor of the Lord, that is, with his identity as both authentic human being and true God.

Mary in Apocryphal Literature

During the period when the canon of the New Testament books was being established for the twofold purpose of asserting the authority of the apostolic tradition in and over the church and of excluding all that seemed alien to the deposit of faith, other books that would ultimately be excluded were being composed, read, and recopied by Christians. This literature is described as "apocryphal," that is, "hidden," because it claimed to communicate teaching reserved to a few, or because the reading of them was to be private, not public, or finally because in the worst cases they concealed the truth of the gospels. The Christian apocrypha are far from all of them being heterodox. Rather, in answering questions raised by Christians of the early centuries, they passed on, each in its own manner, this or that idea which these Christians had of Jesus Christ, his apostles, his disciples, and even of his mother. Some of these apocrypha are very old and may attest to Christian traditions that go back to the beginnings of the church.[28]

32. Although Mary is not an important figure in many of the apocryphal works, we cannot ignore the apocryphal traditions if we are interested in the Mother of Jesus from the historical, theological, and liturgical points of view. Not only are a number of them the only early sources (still needing to be studied and clarified) that speak to us of Mary outside of the sacred scriptures, but in addition they fed the piety of the faithful down through twenty centuries of church history.

33. When the *Protevangelium of James* (second half of the second century) tells us that Joachim and Anne were the names of Mary's parents, are we to reject this information as unfounded? Many of the Christian apocryphal writings admittedly delight in turning Mary into a magical figure who has become alien to our faith and piety as modern people. This is the case, for example, with the stories of the child Mary being raised in the Jerusalem temple and receiving her food from the hands of angels[29] and, more generally, with all the texts that develop a real Marian mythology.

34. But when the apocryphal literature tries to provide details that the curious faithful wanted or that seemed necessary in order to support one or another aspect of the doctrine of the incarnation, it no longer shows respect for the mystery. An example: The legend

explaining how Mary's virginity could be attested by the midwife[30] departs in a noteworthy degree from the simplicity with which the gospel speaks of the real and yet extraordinary birth of the Savior. Every Christian must therefore practice a high degree of discrimination in dealing with these legends.

35. Given the quasi-silence of the canonical scriptures, it was the apocryphal writings, using of course a greater or lesser degree of imagination, that provided Christians of the time with missing information about Mary. Combining the several traditions found in those texts, we may say that according to them Mary was of the line of David and was to be born as one free of any and every sin (a condition to be known later as the Immaculate Conception). She was a precocious child and spent her young years in the temple before being given in marriage to Joseph. The apocrypha then dwelt on the annunciation, the birth of Christ, the flight into Egypt, where Mary performed many miracles, the various events in the life of Jesus, whether as child or as adult, in which Mary had a part (at Cana, for example), and on down to the passion and death of Jesus. In addition, some apocryphal texts claim that it was Mary, and not some other woman, who was the first to see the risen Jesus on Easter morning; in the fourteenth century, Gregory Palamas would broaden the claim by saying that she was present at the resurrection of her Son.[31]

36. The apocryphal literature is very sparing of details about Mary's physical appearance; it is content simply to describe her as radiant. At the moral level, she is crowned with all the virtues. She is gentle, thoughtful, zealous. Above all, she is able to use her gifts by humbly applying herself to charitable works. But the apocrypha never mention even the slightest feeling Mary had for Joseph, though he was her husband; the one exception: according to the *History of Joseph the Carpenter,* she too wept at the moment of his death.[32] The psychological picture given of Mary in the apocrypha sometimes makes her, not inhuman, but superhuman.

37. Such are the apocryphal writings; they were drawn upon again, when the time came, in the homilies classed under the general title of *Transitus Mariae* ("Passing of Mary"), which explain the final lot of Mary.[33] On this matter the apocryphal literature is not unanimous. The earliest texts, which do not go back earlier than the sixth

century, know only of the dormition of Mary and say nothing of her assumption, with or without a preceding resurrection. The Orthodox churches prefer to speak of the dormition of Mary, the Catholic Church of her assumption.[34] But in its statements about the assumption the Catholic Church has not cited any text from the apocryphal literature. In fact, however, the apocrypha are often used without being mentioned as such.

38. Some apocryphal writings stressed the divinity of Christ to the detriment of his humanity, which was left to be almost absorbed and to disappear; in this way they upset the admirable balance shown in the Christology of the Chalcedonian Fathers. These texts, or the ideas conveyed in them, could then be used incautiously, especially those having to do with the purity of Mary, her virtues, and the miracles usually ascribed to her. Mary was then looked upon as the mother, no longer of the incarnate God, but of the divinity. For practical purposes, she no longer shared our human condition. But then, what sort of humanity was it that her Son assumed to the point of suffering on the cross and rising on Easter? There is an important theological problem involved here: the salvation of the human race.

MARY IN THE MEDIEVAL CHURCH

39. Beginning in the early Middle Ages, Marian theology and piety concentrated in the person of Mary the realities of both heaven and earth, and did so in language and in titles that were always ambivalent. Thus Mary is, at one and the same time, virgin and *Theotokos,* sister and mother, mother and daughter, parent and child of the Savior. The two natures of Christ are reflected in this symbiosis that henceforth was typical of the veneration of Mary and gave rise to a recurring theological tension. Marian piety became an identifying element in the Christian faith of the early Middle Ages; later on, it became one of the factors in the gradual separation of East and West.

40. This development can be seen in the Marian feasts, which became incresingly important. They had an educational function, namely, to form Christians in the virtues and in the life of the Church. The hymns to Mary were an expression of this catechetical

intention to shape a piety that was alert to the esthetic qualities of the incarnation as represented by the beauty, goodness, and greatness of Mary herself.[35]

41. The iconclast conflict (eighth-ninth centuries) brought to light the tension inherent in this Marian piety: Mary, having become the perfect image of beauty and womanhood, threatened to turn faith in Christ into an idolatrous worship of herself. Strict rules were drawn up in regard to images. Those of Mary were legitimized as objects of veneration but not of adoration, which was reserved to the persons of the Trinity.[36]

42. Unlike the Eastern Churches, which imposed specific limits on Marian iconography, the Western Church gave freer rein to it. While preserving the principal theological motifs, namely, the exaltation of the Mother of God and the veneration of the *Theotokos,* Western piety embraced an abundance of very popular Marian, cultural, and artistic themes, as can be seen in an art in which esthetic elements take precedence over content and its meaning.

43. Beginning in the eleventh century, more and more was written about Marian theology and piety, leading to the assertion: "We can never say enough about Mary!" *(De Maria numquam satis).*[37] But while we acknowledge that Mary deserves more veneration *(doulia)* than all the other saints do, she cannot be an object of adoration *(latria).* Veneration of Mary must be subordinated to adoration of God.

Three main questions, then, seemed to concern theologians on the subject of Mary:[38]

44. a) The first had to do with Mary's situation in regard to sin. Was she born in sin, like every other human creature, or was she not? The question of the immaculate conception thus became a broad theological issue.

In the twelfth century, Eadmer (d. 1124), a Benedictine, wrote a treatise titled *On the Conception of Holy Mary* in which he argued in favor of the immaculate conception. Anselm of Canterbury took the opposite view, as did Bernard of Clairvaux (d. 1153) and Peter Abelard (d. 1142).

In the thirteenth century, Albert the Great (d. 1280) and Thomas Aquinas (d. 1274) emphasized the gap separating Christ and

Mary and maintained that she was purified in the womb of her mother but was not conceived without sin.

45. Other theologians, chiefly Duns Scotus (d. 1308), a Franciscan, defended the thesis of the immaculate conception and made this an increasingly better known idea (whence the title "Marian Doctor" given to Duns Scotus). In the fifteenth century, John Gerson (d. 1429) granted a greater probability to the views of Scotus; as a result, the Council of Basel (1431–39) defined the immaculate conception for the first time:

> "We define and declare that the doctrine according to which the glorious Virgin Mary, Mother of God, due to a special effect of prevenient and operative divine grace, was never really stained by original sin but was always holy and immaculate, is a pious doctrine, conformed to the worship of the Church, the Catholic faith, right reason, and sacred scripture; that it must be approved, maintained, and professed by all Catholics."[39]

This definition was not accepted because of the break that occurred at this point between this conciliarist council and the pope.

46. As reservations were gradually set aside during the fourteenth and fifteenth centuries, the exaltation of Mary, supported now by the assertion of her immaculate conception, turned her into the incomparable "Queen of heaven, glorious Mother of God, immaculate Virgin, worthy of thanksgiving and praise."[40]

47. b) The second of the questions that sum up the Marian concerns of the Middle Ages had to do with her entrance into heaven. Given the fact of the feast of the Assumption, the people of the time asked: "What kind of assumption did Mary experience?" According to Bernard of Clairvaux and Albert the Great, she was received into heaven but without a bodily ascension; she died and was then raised to the empyrean, the heavenly abode of the saints and the humanity of Christ. Although some theologians, such as Fulbert of Chartres (d. 1208) and Bernardine of Sienna (d. 1444), defended a bodily assumption, it can hardly be said that this was an acknowledged theme of medieval theology and devotion.

48. c) The third question that preoccupied the Middle Ages was the role Mary played on behalf of believers both on earth and in

heaven. The question had its starting point in the words "full of grace" in Luke 1:28.[41] As queen of heaven, Mary was regarded as transmitting the merits of Christ to believers; around the year 1100 this idea found expression in such hymns as *Salve Regina* and *Ave, Regina coelorum.* She concerned herself primarily with the most wretched of the people on earth; she was the mother of mercy (mater misericordiae), our hope, and our advocate. To the extent that medieval Christology looked on Christ primarily as judge, Mary became "reconciler of the world" (Anselm of Canterbury), or even "savior" (Bridget of Sweden, d. 1373; Denis the Carthusian, d. 1471), although these notions did not receive any dogmatic backing.

49. It was thought that Mary could obtain many graces, and even the Holy Spirit, for believers; it was in this sense that she was called *mediatrix* or *cooperatrix* (Bernard of Clairvaux,[42] Denis the Carthusian, John Gerson), but with the reservation that she was strictly subordinate to Christ. It was in this atmosphere that the liturgical hymns and prayers of the time took form, as well as the Marian Psalter (twelfth century), the Marian Office (of John XXII, d. 1334), the Marian Laments (twelfth to fourteenth centuries), and the Office of the Seven Sorrows of Mary (attested since 1324).

50. This Marian piety developed especially in medieval monasticism and was marked by a combination of courtly love for a lady and mystical love for Our Lady. Mary exemplified the service aspect of Christian life, the field in which this idealized love found its application. Cluny began this current of piety, stressing the point, in the person of Peter the Venerable (d. 1156), that Mary is for us a mother of mercy. In the various monastic orders and lay fraternities, from Cluny to the Franciscans and from the Knights to the Beguines, an effort was made to link a life of Christian love with Marian piety in order that mercy might take effective forms.

51. Toward the end of the Middle Ages, certain mariological developments that were at variance with scholastic theology indulged in a piety based on merits and focused on Mary, who became a privileged theme in pictorial and architectural art, pilgrimages, the veneration of images, and stories of apparitions and black virgins.[43] These excesses became increasingly popular and increasingly less controlled

by theology. At the dawn of the Renaissance they would be stumbling stones in the way of various efforts at reform.

THE PROTESTANT REFORMATION AND MARY

52. The development of thought on Mary in the Protestant tradition from the sixteenth to the twentieth centuries can be summed up as follows: In the beginning and in the minds of the reformers, Mary had a relatively important place that was determined by the context of the times. Then this concern for Mary lessened due to confessional controversy, although we find interesting exceptions now and then. In the twentieth century, thanks to the ecumenical dialogue, there was a renewal of interest beginning in the 1920s,[44] an interest that reached its peak in the 1960s (a decade in which some impressive works were published[45]). Beginning in the 1980s there was a new pullback. We must call attention at once to the sometimes notable contrast between the Marian thought of the reformers and the present positions of the churches that sprang from the Reformation.

53. The attitude of the reformers to Mary was an ambivalent one: on the one hand, they defended a polemical position in regard to the Marian piety of the Middle Ages; on the other, they developed a positive interpretation of the person of Mary. It is chiefly in the three major reformers, Martin Luther (d. 1546), Huldrych Zwingli (d. 1531), and John Calvin (d. 1564) that thinking about Mary can be readily seen.

54. Of the three reformers, Luther often speaks of Mary in his writings, and his own piety bore the mark of Marian theology. When he entered the Augustinians, he professed that he would "live his faith to the praise of Mary," but he subsequently revised his Marian theology and Marian piety in light of the antiestablishment themes of his reform; his Marian thinking would be characterized by the same aspects of reform that were found in the other reformers (e.g., the proper conception of faith, salvation, redemption, Christology, and so on). Although he greatly venerated Mary and the saints throughout his life, the matter was always secondary for him; he gave them the place which, in his view, the scriptures allowed him to give them. He

kept three major Marian feasts: the Annunciation, the Visitation, and the Purification.[46] We can discern *six perspectives* adopted by Luther in passages dealing with Mary.

55. First of all, Luther rethought the role of Mary in the light of Christology *(first perspective).* Marian theology must always be subordinated to Christology, and not the other way around. Mary does not have a soteriological role, but is rather a link in the chain of salvation history and a representative of the true condition of believers.

Mary's role is limited, then, to what scripture and the creeds say of her. Luther defends the virginity, and even the perpetual virginity, of Mary[47] and uses metaphors to express and interpret this virginity in a Christological way: she is close to Christ to the extent that she is a sign or metaphor of the incarnation of the Son; she is the place where the mystery of the two natures becomes visible. Her virginity does not give Mary a place apart; quite the contrary, for she is the "Virgin Mary" only thanks to the redemption wrought by Christ. In Luther's view, every believer must be a Christ-bearer no less than Mary, but in a spiritual way.[48] In addition, the reformer criticizes any appeal to Mary's virginity in order to justify any preeminence of virginity generally over marriage.[49]

56. The *second perspective* in Luther's approach to the Marian question concerns her motherhood. No greater praise can be given to Mary than to proclaim that she is the "mother of God."[50] She is by that very fact the instrument of the Holy Spirit, his temple, his "joyous inn." Luther has Mary say: "I am the shop in which he works, but I add nothing to the work; that is why no one should honor or praise me as Mother of God, but should rather praise God and his work in me."[51] In this perspective, Mary is always a historical individual and not someone who is the subject of dogmas.

57. The *third perspective* is ecclesiological. There is an analogy between the destiny of Mary and the destiny of the church: Mary's sufferings remind us of the persecutions of the church; her perseverance, of the continuity and fidelity of the church; her pregnancy, of the way in which Christ the Word comes to dwell in believers. The dignity of Mary finds its expression, paradoxically, in her humility; the same is true of the church, which remains a church beneath the cross, imperfect in its historical, institutional, and visible embodiment.[52] Mary is

thus a figure of the church not only in her motherhood, but also in all the characteristics of her life as attested in the Bible. According to Luther, Mary becomes the mother of each member of the church who has Christ as brother and God as Father.[53] In her role as mother, Mary is also "mother of the church, of which she is also the most pre-eminent member."[54] She is mother of the church of every age, since she is mother of all the children who will be born of the Holy Spirit.[55]

58. The *fourth perspective* has to do with Mary's immaculate conception. Luther studies the question from the angle of "Mary and sin" and of her holiness. The reformer's position on the issue is undecided; he leaves it hanging, because it has no biblical foundation; he says it is a "useless" question.[56] But he applies the same question to Christ: the important thing, he says, is that Christ was born without sin, even while experiencing a real human birth; that is what we ought to believe of him.[57]

59. *Fifth perspective:* the assumption. Luther shows no interest in the traditional way of understanding the question. In his view, it is obvious that Mary is with God, in the communion of saints: "[From the feast of the Assumption of the Virgin] we cannot infer details of the way in which Mary has reached heaven; nor are such details needed, inasmuch as our understanding can never completely grasp everything having to do with the saints in heaven. It is enough for us to know that they are alive in Christ."[58]

At the end of his life he was to preach against this feast, on the grounds that it detracted from the Ascension of Christ.[59]

60. More important in Luther's eyes is the veneration due to Mary, that is, Marian devotion *(sixth perspective).* He examines the veneration paid to Mary in his time, but always in the light of Christology. Mary is indeed "queen!" But the reformer turns the application of the name upside down and extols its seeming opposite: it is only Mary's state as humble servant that expresses her queenship.[60] Her humility found expression in two ways: in her obedience and in her readiness to serve. This twofold humility is the sign of an exemplary faith, which is the way to sanctification. We are therefore to venerate Mary, for when she is thus understood, "all praise of Mary leads to praise of God."[61] Luther does not reject the possibility of an invocation of the saints (that

is, the members of the invisible church, be they living or dead); but he rejects the idea of a mediation of the dead that is won by prayer.

61. The Lutheran position on the question of Mary was approved by Philip Melanchthon (d. 1550). In his *Defense of the Confession of Augsburg* (1531), Melanchthon affirms anew the necessary christocentric character of all thinking about Mary. Mary is not to be regarded as Christ's equal, as she was in the Marian excesses of the medieval church, but is to be venerated because of the example she gave.[62] This proviso having been set down, Mary is seen in the Lutheran tradition as "pure," "holy," a "virgin,"[63] worthy of the greatest praise,[64] and it is as such that she prays for the church. The veneration of Mary casts light on the veneration which Christians owe to all the saints: we ought to remember them, thank God for what they were, take them as models of faith, honor them, and "bear witness to our love for them in Christ,"[65] because they are examples of the mercy of God.

62. Zwingli likewise gives Mary a place which, however, later Zwinglian Protestantism would forget. He has a great deal to say about her as he justifies a piety that venerates Mary but does not adore her. He preserves many of the external forms of Marian devotion: the feasts of the Annunciation, the Assumption, and Candlemas, the ringing of the Angelus, the biblical section of the Hail Mary (the prayer as a greeting, therefore, but not as an intercession). In the setting of his own Christology this reformer of Zurich assigns more importance than Luther does to the virginity. The entire mystery of the incarnation is linked to this perpetual virginity.[66]

63. The theme of Mary as mother occurs less frequently in Zwingli. In his view, Mary is more receptive than bestowing; she is the "house of God," the "safe place" and "chamber" of the Holy Spirit.[67] The Zurich reformer does speak from time to time of Mary as *theotokos*, "Mother of God" and "Mother of Christ" or, again, as "the one who gave birth to our salvation," but he rejects a figurative or dogmatic interpretation of this motherhood, which in his view is simply a historical fact and does not entail any function as mediatrix or cooperatrix.

64. Mary is not holy of herself, but only through and in Christ. Thus the immaculate conception is automatically rejected; the question has no relevance to the Bible. If Mary is said to be "pure" or "spotless," it is because of her exemplary faith and obedience, which

make of her the model believer, and not because of a sinless conception. Mary's holiness always depends on Christ: Mary is "a type of Christ"; in this sense, she is holy on the basis of her historical role and not prior to it. Oddly enough, Zwingli kept the feast of the Assumption in Zurich in view of popular devotion rather than of Marian theology. But the ecclesiological theme of Mary as mother of the church is nonexistent in Zwingli. On the other hand—and this is something original in relation to the other reformed traditions—Zwingli takes over the medieval theme of Mary as model of ecclesial ministry: Marian piety should lead the church back to its caritative and social tasks.[68]

65. Calvin is the reformer who has least to say on the subject of Mary. When he comments on the relevant passages of the Bible, he emphasizes the historical dimension of Mary, while also taking over the traditional teaching on her virginity. According to him, she is a "virgin before, during, and after childbirth" *(virgo ante partum, in partu et post partum)*. He lays the emphasis not on the miraculous aspect of Mary's virginity, as Luther does, nor on the moral purity and ministerial role of Mary, as Zwingli does, but on the action of the Holy Spirit in her. Mary is but a particular historical example of what every Christian ought to become. Mary loses her special doctrinal place (1) in comparison with Christ, (2) in comparison with other believers, and (3) in comparison with the church; she retains only her special and certainly unique historical place. Calvin approaches Joseph in the same way, while restoring him to his rightful place alongside Mary.[69] Having transferred Mary's doctrinal importance to the church, he can say that the church is our mother.[70] This shift of importance from Mary to the church reinforces the importance of the theme of motherhood as applied by Calvin to the church. Nevertheless, the title "Mary, mother of the Church," is absent from Calvin; Mary is "blessed" only in her individual status as example for all.[71]

66. Calvin does, however, assign Mary a function of the first rank as former and teacher of salvation and faith.[72] On the other hand, the Genevan reformer refuses the title "Mary, mother of God," whether because of confessional polemics or for pedagogical reasons. It is on didactic grounds that Calvin's Marian theology lays the emphasis on Christ: Mary is called "mother of the Son of God." Here

again, the important thing is not the motherhood of Mary but the divine sonship of Jesus.

67. For Calvin, too, Mary is an ethical model. Her personality disappears behind her role as example; it is this that we must keep before us, without exalting either the historical or the doctrinal person. Mary is a model of listening, understanding, and witnessing. The emphasis is on the manifestation of the virtues exemplified by Mary and on the building up of the Church by these virtues. The community must be urged to imitate Mary, not to adore her.

FROM THE CATHOLIC REFORM TO THE END OF THE NINETEENTH CENTURY

The Catholic Side to the End of the Seventeenth Century

68. Beginning in the period of the Catholic Reform and in its Counter-Reformation trends, Marian theology and piety acquired a new tone, initially with little influence from polemics, but then, beginning in the seventeenth century, increasingly marked by a spirit of controversy as divisions between the churches widened. We need to remind ourselves, however, that the Roman Catholic reform, as expressed in the Council of Trent (1545–63) and in the post-Tridentine period, was basically concerned with other issues: salvation, reform of the episcopal office and diocesan pastoral life, improvement in the training of the clergy, and the sanctification of the faithful. While the place and role of Mary were theologically minor elements in this broad debate, they would nevertheless become Counter-Reformation issues.

69. At the beginning of the confessional controversies, teaching on the Roman side showed an awareness of efforts at reform: as early as the 1520s Augustine Alveld (d. ca. 1535) defended the veneration of Mary against Luther and Erasmus of Rotterdam. John Cochlaeus (d. 1552), Ambrose Catherinus (d. 1553), and Thomas de Vio, known as Cajetan (d. 1534), among others, branded as heretical the theology of Mary as redefined by the Protestant reformers, and they took over the medieval arguments for the Immaculate Conception and the Assumption.[73] Peter Canisius (d. 1597) summarized these in his *Compendium of*

Christian Doctrine (1566), in which he also defended the titles "Queen," "Hope," and "Salvatrix," as well as Marian miracles and the pilgrimages, images, and other manifestations of Marian spirituality.

70. The Council of Trent remained reserved on the subject of Marian theology and practice. In its concern to provide doctrinal definitions in the major areas of disagreement and separation, it approved the Marian practices surviving from earlier centuries (see the *Roman Breviary* of 1568 and the preservation of the traditional feasts) but left definitions to the theologians of the schools; no fundamental dogmatic decree on Mary would be issued until 1854. This reserve explains, in part, the post-Tridentine proliferation of mariological treatises in the different currents of thought within Roman Catholicism. Among those playing a role, in addition to Peter Canisius, already cited, were Jesuits Francis Suárez (d. 1617) and Robert Bellarmine (d. 1621), the "French School" of Pierre de Bérulle (d. 1629), Jean-Jacques Olier (d. 1657), and John Eudes (d. 1680), and many others.

71. At the end of the seventeenth century and during the eighteenth, devotion to Mary and the saints grew at such a rate that later writers would speak of a "Marian century." The joint invocation of "Jesus and Mary" became even more common. The recitation of the rosary helped to the establishment of confraternities focused on Marian piety. Mary was invoked as protector of believers and as victorious in all struggles. A striking example: after the maritime victory won by the Catholic King Philip of Spain at Lepanto in 1570, Pope Pius V inserted the title "Help of Christians" into the litany of Loretto. In addition, he established a new feast of "Our Lady of Victory" as a sign of the gratitude of all Christendom.

72. Mary was henceforth venerated as "Immaculate," "Sorrowful Mother," "Queen of martyrs," "Queen of heaven," "Mother of Good Counsel," "Help of Christians," "Mary of the Victories," "Consoler of the Afflicted," and "Triumphant over Heresy." She became the subject of an increasingly important controversial position taken by the Counter-Reformation in some geographical areas that bordered on the Protestant world (the Tyrol, Bavaria) or in areas with a strong representation of the various confessions (as was then the case with France).

73. At that time, Marian theology and piety played an important part in the pastoral care of pilgrimages. Princes and the clergy,

both secular and regular (with the Jesuits and the Capuchins spearheading the latter), made an extensive contribution as they saw to the development of specifically Marian places: Einsiedeln (where Peter Canisius was living), Altötting (Charles Borromeo), and many others. New churches and chapels were built in these places and dedicated to Mary. The arts that found expression in them (architecture, painting, music) contributed to the blossoming of this kind of piety. Meanwhile, beginning in the sixteenth century, "Congregations of the Blessed Virgin" were established; in 1576 these already had almost thirty thousand members.

74. As an indirect result, the saints closely associated with Mary, Joseph in particular, also profited and acquired a new status: in 1621, the feast of St. Joseph was declared a holy day in territories under Roman obedience; St. Anne received an official feast beginning in 1623. These were signs of the increasing importance of the men and women saints who were close to the Virgin in one or other of her roles. The Counter-Reformation aspect of this Mariology could be seen in the fact that "new converts" were called up to give evidence of their return to the Roman Church by acts of explicitly Marian piety.

75. Beginning with the Thirty Years War (1618–48) and the fierce interconfessional struggle associated with it, these tendencies developed further and then were strengthened both in their importance and in their exaggerations (this on the Catholic side; Protestants reacted either with caution or in a spirit of excessive reductionism). Mary was the intermediary who eased the Christian journey; believers were called upon to consecrate themselves wholly to her (for example, with the "oblation" used in Congregations of the Blessed Virgin), and their spiritual life took a primarily Marian direction.

76. In the excessive forms of Marian piety a certain (competitive) parallelism with Christology could be seen; for example, in the "Mary-like" life of Carmel, there was talk of a way of living "in Mary," a "loving breathing of the soul toward Mary," to the point that the souls of believers were "formed in Mary," while Mary "lived in the soul and did everything in it."[74] This kind of parallelism recalls, among other things, the "joyful exchange" of conjugal love between Christ and the believer that was prized by Luther. On the other hand, this Marian mysticism did not exert a determining influence, even if

some elements of it were to appear in other forms, for example, in "enslavement to Mary."[75] Unlike Marian mysticism, this devotion, marked by "a loving readiness to serve the Mother of God" and a "complete commitment to her service,"[76] did find favorable soil throughout Europe and exerted a considerable influence there.

77. Beginning in the seventeenth century, that is, on the threshold of the modern age, in this area as in others and in all the churches without distinction, there was a widening separation between the concerns of an educated elite and those of so-called popular devotion. In the various churches henceforth known as "confessional," a threefold development took place: in the devotion of an elite, in popular piety, and in critical scholarship.[77] On the Roman Catholic side, where it was stimulated by the post-Tridentine pastoral emphasis on evangelization, Marian piety provided the soil for numerous religious practices that were supported by a flowering of mariological writings. This piety was marked by the "religion of the heart" and by affectivity and thus resembled in its forms the Protestant practice of "pietism." The two types of piety were a reaction to the atrocities committed in war by both sides and the terrible miseries that were the result; they were a reaction also to the teachings, felt to be too distant and too intellectualist, of the respective theological orthodoxies.

78. In this environment the new Catholic Marian piety produced growths over which little theological control was exercised; as a result, the Holy Office was obliged to intervene and the Sorbonne to issue censures.[78] There were internal reactions against the exaggerations and deviations, and this not only in Jansenism from the pen of Blaise Pascal (d. 1662)[79] but also from the more authoritative voices of some Jesuits and of the Bishop of Meaux, Jacques Bénigne Bossuet (d. 1704) himself. The latter declares "anathema anyone who denies Mary" and "anathema anyone who belittles her!" but he also denounces the "rash confidence" of those who allow themselves to be "exploited" by "superstitious belief" and the "false piety" displayed in certain Marian practices.[80] Still others, such as Bishop Antoine Godeau (d. 1672), at the time when the Jansenist quarrel was most intense, raised their voices against "the incense of excessive praise" that was being offered to the Virgin and against "false miracles," "undisciplined devotions," and hymns that "offend her."[81]

79. These tensions led to a real Marian crisis, which Louis-Marie Grignion de Montfort (d. 1716), to give one example, sought to resolve while taking into account the criticisms coming from all sides: from the Protestants, on the one hand, and from the Jansenists and authoritative theologians on the other.[82] In response to the suspicions of some, there was an effort to make the veneration of Mary less dubious; in response to the exaggerations of others, there was an effort to make it more Christocentric. One of the most popular works of the time, *The Mystical City of God* (1670) by Spanish Franciscan Maria de Agreda, was so larded with legends and theological aberrations on the life of Mary that Pope Innocent XI had to prohibit the reading of it in 1681.

80. We must, of course, always bear in mind the polemical aspect of these Mariological disputes: their excesses and deviations must be interpreted in the context of the exacerbated confrontations of the time. It would, however, be an anachronism to see the situation as already a central element in interconfessional disagreements. For while Marian practices elicited Protestant gibes, the doctrine was not yet a determining point of contention: neither side, and not even the Huguenots, doubted the legitimacy of the role and the "mystery" of the Mother of the Lord.

The Protestant Side in the Sixteenth and Seventeenth Centuries

81. In the period of the Edict of Nantes (1598–1685) confessional coexistence in all its geographical breadth was also, in France, a rare case of religious duality. As least in theory and in law, if not in practice, there was confessional equality, not confessional tolerance: Roman Catholics and Reformed Catholics[83] lived under a single monarch; the coexistence of the two was a permanent reality. The division was not yet seen as inescapable; confessional consciousness had not yet replaced the consciousness of oneness; proximity was still strong enough that intense controversy was seen simply as one of the conditions of life for the respective ministries.[84] On the Protestant side, how did this proximity within a divided unity make itself felt in the area of Marian controversy?

82. We saw earlier that the Protestant reformers of the sixteenth century had much more positive ideas about Mary than did their

descendants of the nineteenth and twentieth centuries. In contrast, the reformed positions in the seventeenth century remained in the line of the original reformers, while at the same time not undergoing developments of practice parallel to those in Roman Catholicism; the scriptural principle prevented any Marian movement beyond what Luther and his contemporaries maintained and acted on. But that principle stated a minimum necessary, and Marian developments beyond that point, although open to challenge, did not justify a reactionary indifference. What could be said of Mary in keeping with *sola Scriptura* was sufficient for anyone who wanted to remain faithful to the Reformation.

83. Reformed theologian Charles Drelincourt (d. 1669) provides an exemplary instance of that fidelity. Far from being a marginal figure, this pastor of the Reformed Church of Paris was one of the most respected and celebrated men of his generation. He was a formidable controversialist and achieved fame beyond the confines of his confessional church. In 1633, he published a short treatise (reissued in 1643) titled *The Honor Due to the Holy and Blessed Virgin Mary.*[85] Given the author's audience, the teaching he presents can be regarded as the authoritative thought of the Reformed theologians and faithful of his time. Drelincourt's purpose was to refute "the most widespread calumny against us, that we dishonor the Blessed Virgin and speak of her with scorn."

84. According to Drelincourt, Reformed Christians profess Mary to be "Virgin," "Blessed," and "one who remained a virgin even in and after giving birth." "With the ancients," they acknowledge her to be "the Mother of God," "forever blessed," and "resplendent with virtues." She was "favored beyond all the patriarchs, prophets, and apostles, and exalted above all the angels and seraphim."

As for the devotion which every Reformed Christian should have toward her, it "is evident that the Holy and Blessed Virgin ought to be loved and honored by all Christians" and that all Christians ought to "venerate her memory, celebrate her praises with exceptional delight," praise God "for the gift received in her," "follow all the teachings which the Holy Spirit has left us through this instrument of grace," "offer her as an example of right living and right belief," and "extol her blessedness and happiness."

85. In contrast to Roman theology, Drelincourt refuses the attribution to Mary of the titles "Infanta," "Queen," "Empress," and "Regent of paradise." One commits "the crime of *lèse-majesté*" when one "renders her honors that belong to the king alone." He alone is "the true gate, our advocate, the sole mediator between God and humanity." It is at that point that the Protestant criticism of Mary applies, that is, where there is danger of Christological distortion: "Not only would we offend our Lord Jesus Christ, but we would also dishonor the Holy Virgin herself."

86. The extreme sobriety of Reformed Marian piety was intended as a safeguard against idolatry. According to Drelincourt, Protestants do not celebrate the Marian feasts or pray the Hail Mary, even if "the words of it are excellent," because "the use of all these is wrong." We would "very grievously offend the Holy Virgin if we believed that she can take pleasure in ceremonies such as unfortunate idolaters invented in the past in the service of their false gods." God "has not sent us to her," and we ought not to pray to her or ask her help but only to praise her. Drelincourt ends by saying: "In all our afflictions we have the Most Holy Trinity as our refuge."

The Catholic Side from the Eighteenth Century to the End of the Nineteenth

87. In the eighteenth century, after a time of infatuation, Marian theology entered into a period of somewhat greater calm, although the influence of the seventeenth century continued to be seen in some characteristics of the new age. There were calls for mitigations and corrections. Thus in 1714 Italian historian Ludovico Antonio Muratori (d. 1751) published a work (in Latin) with the title *On Restraint in Religious Thought.*[86] He attacks the ritual, introduced by the Sorbonne and spread abroad, especially in Spain, of the "blood vow," that is, a vow to defend the Immaculate Conception even to the point of martyrdom. He regards this as a "superstition to be avoided" and reminds his readers that according to the scriptures Jesus Christ is the sole mediator, that only devotion to Christ is necessary for salvation, and that the invocation of the saints and the Virgin, however useful, cannot be called necessary. In many parts of the church, these views

were called scandalous, but when they were brought before the Congregation of the Index, they met with an extremely favorable judgment (in 1753). This was proof that the most official theological authority approved such efforts at restoring moderation.

88. When confronted with the rationalism of the Enlightenment, Marian theologians sought to maintain what was essential. This was true in particular of Alphonsus Maria de Liguori (d. 1787), founder of the Redemptorists and author of, among other writings, a *Dogmatic Treatise against the So-called Reformers* (1769) and, earlier, of a defense of the *Glories of Mary* (1750). He asserts once again that Mary is the necessary channel of all graces, because her role is essentially that of the "Mother of mercy." In this role she rescues sinners from condemnation and prepares the way of salvation for them. But, despite this kind of reaffirmation, rationalism caused a clear moderating of Marian theology and even of Marian piety; thus some bishops had images removed and reduced the number of Marian shrines. The papal suppression of the Jesuit Order in 1773 also played a part, as did pre-Revolutionary ideas.

89. The nineteenth century and the period of the Catholic Restoration brought a new flowering of Marian piety, especially in the form of an abundant popular literature. A new "Marian century" (from 1850 to 1950) was on the way: its dominant characteristics were a revival of pilgrimages, the phenomenon of apparitions (at Lourdes in particular), and doctrinal claims. At mid-century (1854), the dogma of the Immaculate Conception emerged as one of the high points of this development; the dogma of the Assumption was on the distant horizon (1950).

90. The religious restoration and renewal of the nineteenth century paved the way for the doctrinal and magisterial affirmation of a Marian theology that had been lived out for centuries and had gradually taken a fixed form. The agreement within the church between the theology of the schools and popular piety, between the institutional hierarchy and the people of the (Roman Catholic) Church called for a magisterial statement that reflected this consensus. The Marian setting made this statement possible.

91. The claims uttered long ago by medieval Franciscan Duns Scotus, that the Immaculate Conception brought into unity the dogmatic

truths of original sin and saving grace, now provided the basis for a consensus leading to a definitive affirmation. The appearance of the Virgin in 1830 to Catherine Labouré (d. 1876), a Daughter of Charity and an ordinary servant in Paris, together with the "miraculous medal" that came with the Virgin and carried the inscription "O Mary, conceived without sin, pray for us who have recourse to you," played a role in this establishment of dogma.

92. When Pius IX, who was known for his devotion to Mary, became pope in 1846, he hastened the process, for at the urgent request of the North American bishops, he authorized the appointment of Mary as patroness of the United States. In 1848 he appointed a first commission of nineteen theologians to answer the question whether the Immaculate Conception of Mary could be proclaimed a dogma. After consulting with the bishops in 1849, Pius IX solemnly proclaimed the long debated and often challenged definition of the Immaculate Conception, thus making it an obligatory part of the faith.

93. On the whole, the new dogma was well received in the Catholic world. Its proclamation served to give Roman Catholicism a more united front. For the Churches of the Reformation and for Orthodoxy, however, the dogma became an added stumbling block. It would play a part in removing from Protestant piety the remaining traces of the Marian reflection and piety of the Reformers.

MARY IN THE TWENTIETH CENTURY

In the Catholic Church

94. Three main stages can be seen in the history of the twentieth-century Catholic Church, with the Second Vatican Council marking a major break: from the beginning of the century to the Council; the Council as a turning point; the directions taken after the Council.

FROM THE BEGINNING OF THE CENTURY TO VATICAN COUNCIL II

95. Marian theology and piety continued to develop due to the momentum of nineteenth-century fervor. There was a constant competition between piety and dogmatic reflection.

96. On the side of piety, there was an extension of the phenomenon of apparitions as compared with the nineteenth century (Fatima is still the most famous). But the Catholic religious authorities "recognized" only a small number of them. Pilgrimages to Marian shrines, local or national, were very crowded. Many congregations and associations placed themselves under the patronage of Mary (e.g., the Legion of Mary, founded in Dublin in 1921). Marian fervor played a large part in the pastoral handling of popular religion. Mary was taken as the model of women and of mothers in particular. The simple language she used in the New Testament and in messages during her apparitions was more eloquent than many doctrinal sermons.

97. In liturgy and theology we witness a development in which the basic concern was to labor to an ever greater extent for the glory of Mary. New Marian feasts were established. Marian congresses multiplied in which popular manifestations and spiritual conferences were combined. These were often the occasion for the expressions of wishes for the progress of Marian teaching: for dogmatic definitions of the Assumption, of Mary's universal mediation, of her coredemptive role, and for the establishment of new feasts. Then, too, beginning in 1935 societies of Marian studies were founded for the purpose of glorifying the Blessed Virgin and gaining a deeper understanding of her mystery. The term "Mariology" was coined around that time, it seems, and showed that thought about Mary was becoming an autonomous area of theology. An extensive range of subjects was tackled, and a set of concepts, taken indeed from Scholasticism but new in their application to Mary, was used in an effort to give dogmatic status to her mystery.

98. It was under Pius XII that this Marian movement reached its high point. In 1942, during the Second World War, the pope consecrated the world to the Immaculate Heart of Mary, in keeping with the vow he sent to Fatima. More important, on November 1, 1950, he solemnly defined the Assumption of Mary to be a revealed dogma of faith. This placed a new major difficulty in the way of ecumenical dialogue.

VATICAN COUNCIL II

99. Vatican Council II represented a turning point in doctrinal, spiritual, and pastoral thinking about Mary. The Council met at a time

when the trends just described were still to a large extent shared by the conciliar fathers. A number of them, therefore, expected the Council to issue a new Marian definition, or at least a proclamation of new titles for Mary. ("We must add new precious stones to her crown.")

But a different trend increasingly manifested itself, one that voiced its reticence in the face of what it regarded as "Marian inflation." Against the tendency to assimilate Mary as much as possible to Christ (*christotypic* orientation), the other group, which was concerned for both doctrinal balance and ecumenical openness, reminded the fathers of the need to bring Mary back into the church of the redeemed (*ecclesiotypic* orientation).[87]

100. The latent crisis came to a head in connection with a decisive vote: was the Council to produce a document devoted exclusively to the Virgin Mary or was it to introduce the subject of Mary in a chapter of the Constitution on the Church? The Council was divided into two almost equal groups; there was a plurality of only forty votes in favor of the second alternative. This vote, which was experienced as a moment of drama, showed a desire to halt the Marian movement as it had thus far been developing, and a concern to return to a Marian theology based on the scriptures, a theology that would be more sober in its expression, more solidly based on doctrine, and would give Mary her true place in the mystery of salvation as a whole.

101. The original draft document was therefore completely rewritten with the deliberate intention of locating "Mary in the mystery of Christ and of the Church"; the new text became the last chapter of the Constitution on the Church. The Council thus moved from a Mariology that was autonomous and dangerously cut off from the rest of theology, to a teaching on Mary that was integrated with theology in its entirety and, in this sense, functional.

102. Chapter VIII of *Lumen Gentium* was written with great moderation. It makes scripture the basis of the exposition and follows the plan of salvation from the slow preparation for Christ's coming to the glorification of Mary, while tracing the course of her life and taking as its starting point such prophecies as refer to her. The document deals not in biblical exegesis properly so called but in a biblical theology that relies on a body of scripture that is carefully limited to indisputable texts. The document also draws on the teaching of the church fathers

and takes over the content of established dogmas. At the same time, however, it deliberately avoids the concepts and subjects discussed in the "Mariology" of the first half of the century. It intends neither to produce any new definition nor to settle any ongoing disagreements. In her role in the incarnation and in redemption Mary is described as an "associate" and as a humble servant whom the grace of God has allowed to "cooperate" in salvation by her obedience, her pilgrimage of faith, her hope, and her love, from her fiat at the Annunciation to the "consent" she gave to the cross. Finally, the text emphasizes the connection of Mary with the church, of which she is a figure (type) and the most outstanding member and in which she has a maternal role.

103. Pope Paul VI, for his part, on grounds of his personal authority and independently of the Council, was eager to proclaim Mary as "Mother of the Church, that is, of the entire people of God, including both faithful and pastors." This proclamation was by no means a dogmatic definition.

SINCE VATICAN II

104. The Council was followed, initially, by a period of relative silence about Mary. Marian theology took a critical look at itself before following along the line set by the Council. The Council's two major themes—Mary in the plan of salvation and Mary in the church—provided the basic problems. Marian theologians, by and large, moved from a theology of Mary as queen to a theology of Mary as servant. The day of a "triumphalist Mariology" seemed to be over. Also to be seen was the emergence of thought about the relationship of Mary to the Holy Spirit.

105. On the other hand, the devotion of the Catholic people to Mary continued. It is striking that, given the extensive fall off in religious practice since Vatican II, attendance at Marian pilgrimages has remained the same where it has not increased.

106. Pope Paul VI published two documents on the Virgin Mary that were in the line set by Vatican II.[88] The second of them can be regarded as a "directory" of Marian devotion as outlined by Chapter VIII of *Lumen Gentium*.

107. John Paul II has a deep personal devotion to Mary, whom he mentions at the end of all his addresses. He has visited the great Marian shrines of the world. His most important doctrinal statement about

Mary is the encyclical *Redemptoris Mater* (1987), which, in its essential lines, follows the conciliar document, citing it sixty-seven times. In this work the pope emphasizes his ecumenical intentions, with regard especially to Orthodoxy. His meditation on Mary is deliberately based on the Bible and legitimately applies to Mary the key passages of St. Paul on election, grace, and justification by faith. Mary's faith, which is strongly emphasized, is compared with that of Abraham.

108. In its third section, on the "maternal mediation" of Mary, the encyclical does, however, introduce some variations on *Lumen Gentium*. Whereas the Council had deliberately turned away from the term "mediatrix," using it only once in a list of expressions that describe the intercession of Mary, the pontifical document introduces the expression "maternal mediation" as an important concept in Marian theology. The words are doubtless explained in a way that removes any ambiguity. The pope's thought starts from the New Testament text and the Pauline tradition that proclaims Christ to be the "one mediator" (1 Tim 2:5), and it keeps coming back to this as its touchstone. Mary's "mediation" is then described as *participated* and *subordinate*, as a *maternal* mediation that is implemented through *intercession*. It is thus not in any sense of the same order as that of Christ. But, in light of these precautions, one may ask: Is it appropriate to use a term that calls for so many explanations and justifications to ensure its being "correctly understood" in a very analogous sense, especially since it obviously creates difficulties for Christians who are descended from the Reformation?

109. The directives of Vatican II remain in force today. But in some theological circles we also see the reappearance of Marian trends predating Vatican II. We also sense that in some strata of the Catholic people there is being born a nostalgia for traditional Marian piety. People, especially from traditionalist groups, have begun again to frequent controversial places of apparitions, despite the stern warnings of bishops. At the same time, however, we must also acknowledge the effort being made at some important places of pilgrimage (Lourdes, La Salette, etc.) to foster in the pilgrims an experience of faith that is authentic and formative. Nowadays, these pilgrimages are privileged places for the exercise of a Catholic pastoral oversight of popular Christianity.

In the Churches Descended from the Reformation

110. Given the ongoing and, in their view, inordinate development of "Mariology" in the Roman Catholic Church, the Churches of the Reformation have felt increasingly obliged to react strongly against the cult of Mary and the teaching which undergirds it and which Karl Barth looked upon as a "heresy," a "malign growth," a "greedy branch" of theological thought.

111. No one doubts that the promulgation of the dogma of the Assumption (1950), coming as it did after that of the Immaculate Conception (1854), represented a high point in the hardening of interconfessional relations and that it gave rise to a real outcry in the other churches, where the news was received with dismay.[89] There was a sense abroad that the age-old gulf between the Church of Rome and these other churches had once again been widened, to the point now of becoming unbridgeable, and this at the very time when the ecumenical movement was gaining strength in other areas.

112. At the time of the Second Vatican Council, the Churches of the Reformation welcomed with interest, on the one hand, the reluctance of the Council fathers to give Mary the title of Mediatrix (an idea that unfortunately reappeared in the encyclical *Redemptoris Mater* of 1987) and their refusal of the title Coredemptrix and, on the other hand, their attempt to draft a "Christology of Mary." The inclusion of Marian teaching in the dogmatic Constitution on the Church *Lumen Gentium* and the concomitant refusal to devote a separate conciliar text to it, were understood by Protestants as evidence of the Council's concern not to continue creating an autonomous Mariology that would be separate from the theology of the mystery of salvation and have its own special status, analogous and parallel to Christology. They saw the Council as deciding, instead, to incorporate any thought about Mary into the mystery of the church by centering it more fully in Jesus Christ, the one and only mediator.

113. From the Protestant viewpoint, this effort of the Council to recenter everything in Christ did not answer the difficulties still raised by the official Marian teaching of the church. There were at least two reasons for this:

The first has to do with the scriptural basis of the teaching. Neither the dogma of the Immaculate Conception nor that of the bodily assumption of the Virgin Mary have a credible biblical foundation. They are justified solely by arguments from tradition or an appeal to doctrinal consistency. How then can one accept a teaching presented as a truth of faith when it is not rooted in the scriptures? The second reason, which overlaps the first, has to do with human cooperation in the work of salvation.[90]

114. The Reformation Churches, today as in the past, refrain from giving Mary a place other than her proper one, the one assigned her by the angel. In the name of fidelity to the apostolic witness and in the name of the respect and affection they have for the Mother of the Lord, they strongly resist any effort to exalt Mary and to establish a parallelism between her and Christ or between her and the church by bestowing on her titles which, in their eyes, distort her rather than attest to her true being. In such a Mary they no longer see the "little Mary" of the gospel, "our sister."[91]

115. There is then no "Mariology" in the churches of the Reformation, nor any Marian devotion, that is, neither Marian services nor prayer to Mary. On the other hand, we can see taking place a renewed reflection on Mary. Set against the background of the great Christological statements of the early ecumenical councils (especially Ephesus and Chalcedon) and the writings of the sixteenth-century reformers, this reflection takes the form of resituating the Mother of God in the mystery of salvation and seeing her as humble servant and admirable witness to the faith and as the foremost of redeemed creatures. We can likewise see developing a piety that, fed as it is by the gospel, pays increasing heed to the praise-filled faith of Mary that is so well expressed in the Magnificat.

116. A development along these lines can be seen in the liturgies, hymns, and catechisms of the Lutheran and Reformed Churches of France from the end of the nineteenth century down to our day.

117. Whereas in the nineteenth century the person of Mary, along with mention of the communion of saints, was practically absent, a place has gradually been made for them in the course of the twentieth.

During this period, the catechisms used in the named churches have devoted more or less lengthy chapters to a determination of what Protestants believe and do not believe about Mary. Here is a revealing extract from a catechism:

> She is the servant of God par excellence. God chose and called her from among all women to be the mother of his Son. In contrast to Eve, who chose the path of disobedience, Mary answered her call with faith and humility. We find her again beneath the cross and in the first community of disciples (Acts 1:14). Her most beautiful words are contained in her canticle, the Magnificat (Luke 1:46–55).

In regard to the Virgin Mary, the Evangelical Church believes everything that is written about her in the Bible; this means that we not believe:

> –in her immaculate conception, that is, her miraculous birth [sic[92]] from a legendary mother, Anne;
> –or in her assumption, that is, her bodily ascent into heaven (celebrated on August 15);
> –or in her participation in the work of salvation, something of which the Bible says nothing.[93]

All the catechisms do, of course, devote pages to the second article of the Apostles' Creed: "who was conceived by the Holy Spirit and born of the Virgin Mary," when speaking of the divine and human natures in Jesus Christ.

118. Beginning in the 1960s, the renewal of Protestant Christology on the one hand, and the ecumenical movement on the other, led to many references being made to Mary in hymns and the liturgy. Two characteristics are to be noted: the restraint of these references and the often explicitly indicated biblical basis. The references focus on Mary's answer to the angel, her obedience, her faith, her remembering, and her excellence as mother. It is more especially in the seasons of Advent and Christmas, and in texts for the Eucharist and for adoration,[94] that she is named and seen as one of the communion of witnesses from all times and places. Nor is it a matter of indifference that six variations on the Magnificat are included for liturgical use in

the hymnal *Arc-en-Ciel* (1988), which is widely used in liturgical assemblies; earlier, there were only two in *Nos coeurs te chantent* (1969), one in *Louange et Prière* (1939), and none in *Sur les ailes de la foi* (1926).

119. The discussion of the Virgin Mary makes it clear that today she is perhaps the point at which all the underlying confessional differences, especially in soteriology, anthropology, ecclesiology, and hermeneutics, become most clear. These issues are fundamental, if any are, so that when all is said and done, the ecumenical dialogue on the Virgin is a suitable locus for ascertaining our doctrinal disagreements, as it is a no less suitable locus for looking self-critically at our respective ecclesial behaviors in regard to the Mother of the Lord.

2

The Testimony of Scripture and the Confession of Faith

120. ◆ The three articles of the creed[1] will provide the outline for our doctrinal reflections on Mary. We are not forgetting, of course, that the creeds deal first and foremost with the Trinity and its manifestation in the economy of salvation, which climaxes in the event that is Jesus Christ. It is not our intention, moreover, to comment on all that is said in the creed. We want simply to grasp Mary's proper place in a whole that is far greater than she and in the service of which she has been placed. Mary ought never to be considered in isolation.

121. The first article confesses God as the almighty Father and creator of all things. Mary is one of his creatures.

The second article is devoted to the human journey of Jesus Christ, the Son of God, who came "for us men and for our salvation." This article mentions Mary as his mother.

The third article speaks of the Holy Spirit and of the church that he sanctifies. Mary is a member of this church and belongs to the communion of saints.

FIRST ARTICLE: MARY: CREATURE, WOMAN, AND DAUGHTER OF ISRAEL

122. In our desire to bring out the humanity of Mary we take from the scriptures everything that can shed light on the human,

cultural, and religious roots that make Mary a "woman of our world," a "daughter of Israel," and a "spouse" and a "mother."

A Woman of Our World

123. The first article of the creed professes God to be "the Father almighty, creator of heaven and earth, of all that is seen and unseen." Mary, for her part, is fully a part of this created world. She cannot be likened to the goddesses worshiped in the religions of antiquity. She is not outside or above the human race, but belongs entirely to the human race with which God willed to crown his creation.

124. It is as a woman that Mary should first be considered—not, however, as a woman separated from other human beings nor as a model of passive submission which other women adopt in their relations with men, or as a symbol of an ideal femininity that would imply some scorn of sexuality and fleshly generation. These are deviations legitimately pointed out by feminist thought in our time, but they have too often characterized representations of Mary down the centuries. The development of modern art shows that while such painters as Georges de la Tour have wonderfully captured the silent interiority of Mary, who could then be seen as a "sublimated" image of woman, other artists have "idealized" Mary, who then runs the risk of being a mere projection of an imaginary desire or the expression of an idolatrous deviation.[2] We understand better today that such representations were very ambiguous and could stand in the way of the original gospel witness about the mother of Jesus. She was, in fact, a woman among women, a woman of our world, a woman who, like many others, experienced the two states of wife and mother.[3]

125. History also bids us recognize the fact that, despite the abuses contained in one kind of Mariology, meditations on Mary have also contributed to a better understanding of women and their role in society. In particular, Mary is the woman to whom many of the poor have turned, looking to her for strength and comfort. People have been aware of her human and maternal closeness to them; they have spontaneously recognized the face of tenderness and compassion; they have remembered her amid the joys as well as amid the sufferings of life. Today as in the past, many see in the mother of Jesus a woman

who is "one of us," a creature of God who truly belonged to the "poor ones of Israel," and whose very human face continues to shine forth in the faith and hope of the humble.

A Daughter of Israel

126. The fact that Mary was human means that she belonged to a particular people: the Jewish people. As a woman, she did not have a special place in the social or religious life of that people. She was in no way comparable to Miriam, the sister of Moses (Num 26:59), who had played an important role in the leadership of the Jewish people (Exod 15:20; Mic 6:4); nor was she in any way comparable to other Old Testament prophetesses such as Deborah in the period of the Judges (Judg 4–5) or to heroines such as Judith and Queen Esther who made possible the deliverance of their people and were thus instruments of divine justice. Mary did not play any special role among her people. She was an ordinary woman, and her name was common enough that other women of the same name in the gospel had to be distinguished by their relatives or their place of origin (the sister of Martha; the wife of Clopas; Mary of Magdala, and so on). Does not the matter-of-factness of the gospel stories suggest in their own way the very ordinary state of this woman whom Péguy would one day describe as "a poor Jewish woman of Judea" and "the humblest of creatures"?

127. It was as a woman of her people that Mary experienced both her virginity and her motherhood. The Old Testament had earlier spoken of the virginity of Rebekah: "The girl was...a virgin, whom no man had known" (Gen 24:16). Then, too, the Law prescribed that the high priest must marry a virgin (Lev 21:13). The word "virgin" also served to describe the people of Israel ("virgin daughter Zion": 2 Kgs 19:21) or even another people ("virgin daughter Babylon": Isa 47:1). But the word was in fact used ambivalently: a virgin was one who could be given in marriage, but she was also in danger of being scorned or cursed if, having no husband, she were unable to transmit life. For in the biblical and Jewish tradition virginity was not an end in itself. It was fruitfulness that was regarded as a blessing, as can be seen from the canticle that Hannah sang after the birth of her son, Samuel

(1 Sam 2:1–10). And while "daughter Zion"—that is, the people of Jerusalem or of Judea, whether there or in exile—was compared to a virgin, its call nonetheless was to be the spouse of the Lord and to bear children: "Sing, O barren one who did not bear; burst into song and shout" (Isa 54:1). When, then, Mary became a mother, she took her place in the long line of the women of Israel. She had the experience of childbirth, which ought to crown the life of every woman and contribute to the perpetuation of the chosen people.

128. Not only did Jewish women want to escape barrenness; some of them even hoped to give birth to the Messiah.[4] There is no reason for not thinking that Mary, like others, cultivated that same desire: "Why suppose that Mary did not experience it? When, then, the angel told her the news, was she distressed or even just surprised, as if such a thought had never occurred to her? No! In fact, her joy was so great that she raised no objections as to the father or her husband or her jeopardized honor. Such thoughts vanished when the supreme favor was offered to her. Blessed among women! Blessed indeed!"[5]

129. As a daughter of Israel, Mary made her own the prayer of the women of her people (Luke 1:46-55): such women as Miriam, sister of Moses (Exod 15:20ff.) or Hannah, mother of Samuel (1 Sam 2). On the other hand, she also submitted to the regulations for the various stages of a woman's life. Thus she was legally married to Joseph, even though she did not live with him (Matt 1:18), in accordance with the Jewish requirement of preconjugal virginity. Once she had given birth to Jesus, she, with Joseph, faithfully observed the Jewish rites of birth: circumcision of the child, purification of the mother, dedication of the first-born, offering of a pair of turtledoves or a pair of pigeons (Luke 2:21-24; see Exod 13:2 and Lev 12:1–8). Admittedly, whereas the Jewish law called for the ransoming of the first-born (Exod 13:13), Luke the evangelist speaks of a "presentation to the Lord," and not of a "ransoming" (Luke 2:22); Jesus did not have to be ransomed because (like the Levites, according to Num 3:40ff.) he was to remain the property of the Lord and because he himself was to ransom the multitude. The fact remains, however, that Christ was born of a Jewish woman (Gal 4:4) and was a member of the people to whom belonged "the adoption, the glory, the covenants, the giving of the law, the worship, and the promises...the patriarchs" (Rom 9:4–5). Mary was within

Israel, and Israel within Mary; by that fact, the covenant which God had struck with his people was not withdrawn but was fulfilled in a new way by the coming of "Emmanuel" to the land of Judea.

A Wife and a Mother

130. It is said of Mary that she was "engaged to Joseph" (Matt 1:18). The reference here is to the espousals, which according to Jewish tradition preceded that actual wedding. Later on, when Mary was mysteriously made pregnant, Joseph performed the ritual act that made Mary his wife: "he took her as his wife" (Matt 1:24). The infancy gospels speak of the couple several times: Joseph set out "with Mary his wife" to register as ordered by the emperor (see Luke 2:5); the shepherds found the couple with the newborn child in the stable at Bethlehem (Luke 2:16). According to Matthew, Joseph "took the child and his mother" and withdrew into Egypt (Matt 2:14). According to Luke, the husband and wife went to Jerusalem to present Jesus to the Lord (Luke 2:22) and returned there annually for the feast of Passover (Luke 2:41); then when Jesus was twelve years old, they shared a common grief when they discovered that their child had disappeared (Luke 2:44ff.).

131. One day, a nameless woman in a crowd lifted her voice and said with reference to Jesus: "Blessed is the womb that bore you and the breasts that nursed you!" Luke (11:27). While the Son's response drew attention to the real source of all blessedness ("Blessed rather are those who hear the word of God and obey it"–Luke 11:28), the fact remains that Mary shared the condition of women who have experienced motherhood. She was filled with joy at the announcement of the child to come; she awaited him in patient acceptance of everyday life; she experienced the joy of a mother on first seeing the face of her newborn child. She was familiar with the situation Jesus would one day describe to his disciples: "When a woman is in labor, she has pain, because her hour has come. But when her child is born, she no longer remembers the anguish because of the joy of having brought a human being into the world" (John 16:21).

132. Beginning on the day of his birth and throughout the years that followed at Nazareth, Mary was for Jesus what every Jewish

mother was supposed to be for her child. True enough, according to Matthew it was Joseph, her husband, who gave the child his name, and it was Joseph's role to introduce Jesus to the reading of the Torah, teach him a trade, and gradually prepare him for adult life. But Mary did her part in that work by helping Jesus discover the simple realities of family life and keeping track, as the months passed, of the progress of the child who "grew and became strong" (Luke 2:40). During the time at Nazareth she must have given thought to the future and, like all parents, discussed with Joseph what their son was to become as an adult.

133. The evangelists tell of Mary's joy but they also emphasize her trials and sufferings. When Matthew tells of Mary being pregnant before sharing the life of Joseph, he makes it clear that she could become suspect of infidelity (see Matt 1:18–25). After the birth of Jesus, he speaks of the violence unleashed against the child and his family (see Matt 2).

Luke, for his part, recalls and emphasizes the lowly and uncertain conditions under which Jesus was born: the lack of a place to stay, the birth in a stable (Luke 2:7), the prophecy of Simeon: "A sword will pierce your own soul, too" (Luke 2:35), and, later on during the annual pilgrimage to Jerusalem, the anxiety of a mother who thought her son was lost and who, on finding him, reproached him: "Why have you treated us like this?" (Luke 2:48).

While none of the evangelists says that Mary was pained by her son's departure, the three Synoptic writers do report that Mary and his relatives sought to "see Jesus." Mark adds that they "went out to restrain him, for people were saying, 'He has gone out of his mind'" (Mark 3:21). In speaking thus, Mark is expressing the anxiety of a mother who saw herself and her family humiliated by the skeptical or scornful remarks made about him (see Mark 3:22; 6:1–6). Finally, according to the unanimous tradition of the Gospels, Mary experienced the most terrible trial a mother can endure—that of standing by helplessly at the suffering and death of her own child.

134. We would, then, not be respecting Mary were we not to see in her a true creature of God, a daughter of Israel who shared fully in the history of her people, and a mother who shared the joys and sorrows of motherhood, and all this in everyday existence as well as in the exceptional circumstances of life. It was in and through her human

journey that this woman opened herself to the word of God. It was on that same journey that she was called to believe and learned to become a disciple, step by step, sometimes in light, often in darkness, beginning with the fiat of the annunciation and the exaltation of the Magnificat, and ending in the silent suffering of Calvary.

135. *Such is the profound humanness of Mary. While she extols the Most High because "he has looked with favor on the lowliness of his servant" (Luke 1:48), her Magnificat does not glorify herself but praises the Lord for the wonders he has wrought. If Mary, a woman among women, nevertheless occupies a unique place in God's creation, this place is due to the fact that God chose her to be the mother of his own Son and that she consented unreservedly to this choice.*

We are then respecting Mary when we now turn to the mystery of Jesus Christ who "was born of the Virgin Mary and became a man."

SECOND ARTICLE: MARY, MOTHER OF JESUS: CHRIST, LORD, AND SON OF GOD

136. The second article confesses Jesus to be the Christ and Lord; it names Mary as his mother. In doing so, the creed summarizes at its center the teaching of the New Testament on Mary. The second article thus tells us the place of Mary in God's plan and in the history of salvation.

137. It is in this new setting that we must go back again to the main New Testament passages on Mary and read them in an ecumenical perspective, that is, bringing out what, in our view, belongs to the faith accepted by all.

138. Our intention here is therefore not directly exegetical, although we do want to rely on the most solidly established results of contemporary scholarship. We are not claiming to recover biography and history. We take the texts as they stand in the gospel narrative. Our rereading of the texts will therefore be of a doctrinal and meditative kind.

139. We shall begin with the accounts of the birth and childhood of Jesus in Matthew and Luke; these accounts are not offered as

a more or less faithful review of the memories of Mary and Joseph but rather as an interpretation, in the light of the Easter faith, of the mystery of the coming of the Son of God into the world. We shall then go to the narratives in John, and shall end by recalling the passages in the Synoptics, John, and Acts that have to do with the mother and brothers of Jesus.[6]

The Infancy Gospel according to Matthew (1–2)

140. In these chapters, Mary has a very unobtrusive place and is a passive participant. Although the story does not bring out either the faith or the personal journey of Mary, it does locate Jesus in the history of Israel and, at the same time, shows that the plan of God is being carried out by his coming into the world which God made.

141. Because Jesus of Nazareth was fully incorporated into the human condition in both time and place through his roots in the Jewish people, he had a genealogy. Matthew gives a series of ancestors that in number and duration are symbolic of the fourteen generations from Abraham to David, the fourteen from David to the deportation to Babylon, and the fourteen from the exile to the Messiah. But the uniform repetitions of male progenitors is interrupted four times in order to mention women: Rahab and Ruth, both of them foreigners, are there to show that the rest of the human race is invited to share in salvation along with Israel; Tamar, daughter-in-law of Judah, and Bathsheba, who had been the wife of Uriah before becoming David's wife, are there to remind us that the promise makes its way despite the weaknesses of a patriarch (see Gen 38) and of a king (see 2 Sam 11–12) and, paradoxically, even derives support from them. These four women and the four irregular births that occur due to them prepare the reader for the mention of Mary and for the birth of Jesus, the extraordinary character of which will be brought out later in the narrative.

142. Matthew names, without separating them, the parents of Jesus: Joseph, the husband of Mary (1:16), and, Mary the wife of Joseph (1:24). He thereby shows clearly that like every other child Jesus comes into the world with a father and a mother: the symbolic role of the first complementing the no less symbolic role of the second.

In assigning to Joseph what in Luke is said of Mary (giving of his name to Jesus; revelation by an angel), Matthew cannot be set in opposition to the third gospel. His emphasis in on the Davidic ancestry of Jesus and on the role of Joseph, his full responsibility as head of the family, and his faith in the divine word.

Just as Jesus was not born without identifiable parents, so Mary has no existence apart from Joseph, whose wife she is, and from Jesus, whose mother she is. In chapter 2 of Matthew's gospel the child is always mentioned before the mother (vv. 11, 13, 20, 21).

143. Mary is both begetter and mother, whereas Joseph is only the legal father. This last fact does not, however, make his role less important because, without being a begetter, he is an authentic father and responsible for the human and religious identity of Jesus. The ancestral promises of a Messiah for Israel are thus fulfilled by a virgin mother and an adoptive father. This is the major novelty of this birth when compared with the births in mythology.

144. Matthew is careful to connect his account of "the annunciation to Joseph" with the messianic prophecies and so to bring out the significance of this birth: Emmanuel, that is, "God with us" (1:23; see 28:20), was to be born of a virgin[7]; this birth was to take place at Bethlehem, the royal place of David (2:6); along with his family the child was to experience a kind of nomadic life, after the manner of the patriarch Joseph and his brothers, then of Moses and his people, between the flight into Egypt and a new exodus (2:15).

145. In his concern to locate the humanity of the Messiah in the history of the covenant and as a resident of the "holy" land, Matthew does not answer the questions, ancient and modern, of curious religious minds and suspicious rationalists. The fact that Mary was a virgin when her first child was born is a statement of theological importance about the identity of the Son; it is not an assertion of moral purity about the mother. The important thing was to show respect for a mystery and to call attention to a truly unique birth by means of a sign.

146. The transmission of this first chapter of Matthew shows numerous textual variants that could lead to contradictory views concerning, for example, the virginal birth in v. 25. But there can be no doubt about the central affirmation, which accords with that in Luke: the conception of Jesus took place without male intervention.

147. *All of us confess in faith what we are taught by the infancy gospel of Matthew both about Jesus, the Messiah-Christ, Emmanuel and Savior, and about Joseph, his legal father, and Mary, his virginal mother.*

The Infancy Gospel according to Luke (1–2)

148. Like Matthew, Luke locates Jesus in the history of the Jewish people and emphasizes the new state of affairs that he begins. Mary is the guarantor of his roots, and she is the sign of this newness. She is the first representative of faith in Christ. At the same time, as mother of Jesus she must renounce possession of one who is the Son of God. The faith, which welcomes Christ into her womb, cannot hold on to him who transcends her in every respect. The entire story of the birth of Jesus is, in the final analysis, an invitation to praise the faithful God who is bringing about the salvation of the world through this child.

THE ANNUNCIATION

149. In the Bible, angels personify the messages given by God. In the Old Testament, the angel Gabriel is already the messenger of the good news of the Son of man (Dan 8:16). After having been sent to Zechariah, he comes to tell Mary the good news that will bring her joy.

150. Mary is described as a *parthenos* in accordance with the Greek text of Isaiah 7:14. The word signified, first of all, a young unmarried woman. But it is used here to mean a virgin, and this is confirmed by Mary's objection that she does not "know" any man, that is, that she has not had conjugal relations and that the announced birth will be in fact from a virgin. Mary is, however, said to be espoused to Joseph, a fact that connects her with the posterity of king David.

151. Mary, as a virgin *and* as a mother, is not simply in the line of certain women highlighted by the Old Testament. She is separated from them by the virginal conception, which transforms the meaning both of her virginity and of her motherhood. On the one hand, Mary's virginity is not simply a condition for her marriage to Joseph; she remains a virgin even when she has conceived. On the other hand, the motherhood of Mary cannot be assimilated to the miraculous experience of a barren woman who gives birth: the

marvel here is that Mary gives birth without having known a man.[8] Thus the virginity of Mary does not keep her from being a mother, any more than the fact of being the mother of Jesus calls her virginity into question. This unique situation is due to the plan of God himself who has decided to take flesh, through Mary, within our human history. The fact that the woman on whom the creator Spirit has descended is a virgin is the sign of this decision. Once she had been touched by the shadow of the Most High she became the temple, as it were, of him who through her was coming into the world. Virgin *and* mother: this new reality points to the mystery God has wrought by making Mary, a woman among women, the mother of his own Son.

152. The angel greets Mary as one to whom grace *has been* given: the Lord is with her. The passive expression, "filled with grace," emphasizes the point that grace in Mary is the result of a gift freely given and accepted.[9] This grace is not a thing; it is a quality of her relationship with God, before whom she has "found favor" (1:30).

153. The angel's message gives the child his name: Jesus. This was the name of Joshua, who brought the chosen people into the promised land. It also describes the promised child as Messiah. It adorns him with magnificent titles. Paradoxically, this solemn statement is made to a very simple girl in the obscurity of Nazareth, a village without claim to fame.

154. But all this is not easy, and Mary tries to understand it. Her question compels the angel to speak again. In a new and solemn announcement Gabriel reveals that the child will be the very Son of God. The Spirit, who exercised his creative and life-giving role at the beginning of the world (Gen 1:2), will exercise it again in Mary. No word is spoken here that suggests carnal contact.

155. Once Mary has believed in the angel's words concerning her, she can also believe him when he tells her all that God has done in her cousin. The reference to Elizabeth shows that nothing is impossible to God. One needs only to believe in the promise, and God will give life.

156. In calling herself the *servant* of the Lord, Mary, who was not a servant due to her social status, expresses her readiness to be at the Lord's disposal, but in a free and responsible way. As "the eyes of

a maid" are turned to the hand of her mistress (Ps 123[122]:2), so she places herself at the service of him who will take on himself the condition of a servant (Phil 2:7).

157. *When the Apostles' Creed bids us confess that Jesus, the Christ and the Son of God, "was conceived by the Holy Spirit and born of the Virgin Mary," it summarizes the heart of the message at the annunciation. Mary is named by reason of her part in the mystery of salvation for which she was chosen. Mary, virgin, mother, and servant, goes before us in faith in the incarnate Word.*

THE VISITATION

158. The Visitation shows us how joy and the gift of the Holy Spirit are contagious. Mary has hardly received the angel's message when she hastens to visit her cousin and to experience, together with her, a first outpouring of the prophetic Spirit. Her setting out is also a response of her faith to grace.

159. When Elizabeth hears Mary's greeting, her son, John the Baptist, stirs within her, leaping in gladness, thrilling with happiness (see Luke 6:23); meanwhile his mother is filled with the Holy Spirit and becomes a prophet. The first prophetic human voice to prophesy in the New Testament is that of a woman, just as women will be the first messengers of the resurrection.

160. Elizabeth's prophetic words are, first of all, a blessing. Mary, among all women, is the recipient of a special blessing, one that sees her as the Mother of the Messiah, the supremely Blessed One. Elizabeth also makes her own act of faith, for in the mother of Jesus she already sees the mother of her savior. She then utters the first beatitude, which praises faith: Mary is blessed because she believed that she would become the mother of the Messiah.

161. Mary then recites her Magnificat. Drawing upon the canticle of Hannah (1 Sam 2:1–10) and several statements in the prophets and psalms, it first states something that concerns her personally, but it does so with praise and thanksgiving that are at the same time turned away from her, because what is happening to her is for the sake of the world and will apply from generation to generation. This is why she says that all generations will call her blessed. Here is

the basis of the wonder-filled praise of God that the church of every age is urged to sing in response to the gift which Mary received.

162. The mother of Jesus then celebrates God's justice toward wounded humanity, as well as his fidelity to his people. She reads anew the history of salvation and connects it with what is happening to her. She marvels at the paradoxical plan of God who comes to the aid of the lowly, the poor, and the hungry, in order to bring the promise made to Abraham to fulfillment for them and through them.

163. *The scene of the Visitation bids the church enter into the circle that praises God, with and like Mary and Elizabeth, for the human way in which he comes among us and, together with the lowly, begins the renewal of history.*

THE NATIVITY

164. Up to this point God has directly guided events. From this point on, however, Luke emphasizes the human interventions that will effect the carrying out of the mystery and will subject Mary and Joseph to the testing of their faith. First, there is the edict of Caesar Augustus that compels them to travel. But this very fact shows us that the birth is not a myth, for it occurs at a time and place in universal history, just as the death of Jesus will take place under Pontius Pilate.

165. It is in Bethlehem that Mary delivers her "first-born" Son. This expression locates Jesus within the framework of the Jewish law (Exod 13:15) and looks ahead to his presentation in the Temple. For this infant participates in the privileges and obligations belonging to all first-born males. The expression does not in any way decide whether or not he will remain an only child.[10]

166. Let us note the contrast between the two parts of the scene. There is first of all a report, as sober as could be, on the difficult conditions surrounding the birth of Jesus; so sober is it that we might be reading a news item. Then there is a luminous manifestation of the glory of God (a theophany) and a new revelation communicated by angels.

167. The first sign given to a believer in Christ is a poor newborn child, wrapped in cloths and lying in a manger: this is the distinctive sign of Jesus. Mary and Joseph encircle the child and

present him as object of faith to the shepherds and later to the entire church.

168. Mary, we are told, "treasured all these words and pondered them in her heart" (Luke 2:19). Given the gap between the weakness of the sign and the greatness of the titles bestowed on her Son, she needed to turn into herself and interiorize all that had happened and all the extraordinary things that were said about this little human being who was her Son. She was advancing on her pilgrimage of faith.

169. Eight days later, the child is circumcised in accordance with the Jewish law. He is given the name "Jesus," as prescribed before his conception. The cycle of the birth of Jesus is now complete.

170. *The churches worship this newborn child swaddled and lying in a manger. Amid the weakness, poverty, and lowliness of the creche they bestow on him all the magnificent divine titles: he is Lord to the glory of God the Father. When the ecumenical councils of the fifth century give the name* Theotokos, *"Mother of God," to the servant of the Lord who brought him into the world, they do so not in order to glorify her but primarily to confess that he who was born of her according to the flesh is her Lord and her God.*

THE PRESENTATION OF JESUS IN THE TEMPLE

171. By going up to Jerusalem the first time, in order to present the child in the Temple (Luke 2:22ff.), Mary and Joseph bear witness both to the roots of Jesus in Jewish history and to the fact that he belongs to the Lord. They faithfully obey the rites prescribed by the Mosaic law: the purification of the mother is the consecration of her first-born son.

172. This presentation in the Temple is the occasion of a prophetic revelation, as two elderly people approach the child: Simeon who takes Jesus in his arms and in him sees the salvation of God, and Anna, who praises the Lord and tells everyone around of the child. It is this child who will show himself to be the light of the nations and thereby carry out the vocation of Israel.

173. Simeon also prophesies that Jesus will be a sign of contradiction and that Mary's soul will be pierced by a sword (Luke 2:34–35). The Mother of Jesus is called upon not only to experience the detachment that every mother must cultivate toward her

child; the tragic fate of her Son will have its painful echo within her. Her faith will not keep her from experiencing anxiety or the inability to understand; her faith must grow to endure the trials caused by the revelation of Jesus as Son of God and the paradoxical fulfillment of his mission in the cross, which can already be glimpsed on the horizon.

174. *As it contemplates Jesus in his presentation in the Temple, the church confesses him not only as "the glory of his people Israel" and the "light of the nations," but as one who already has a calling that will lead him to the cross. His mother is made subject, in prophecy, to the same decisive test.*

JESUS LOST AND FOUND IN THE TEMPLE

175. What Simeon the prophet has foretold begins to be fulfilled when the parents again go up to Jerusalem (Luke 2:41ff.). This pilgrimage for the celebration of the Jewish Passover has an unexpected and upsetting outcome. The parents look for their child, who has eluded them, and they tell us, through Mary, of their anxiety and lack of understanding. But when the child is found among the teachers, he reveals himself to Mary and to Joseph, his adoptive father, as the very Son of God, his real Father. He calls his parents to a "conversion": to the recognition of his true identity as one who must be about his Father's business. As at the time of the birth, so now Mary "keeps"[11] these events in her heart, though she does not understand them; this heart is already touched by the sharp sword.

176. *Mary is a woman who must accept the fact that her Son escapes her grasp, in order that she may then accept him for what he really is. She advances in faith through the darkness of trials. The church in turn recognizes in faith that he is first and foremost the Son of the Father.*

The Gospel of John

177. While John the evangelist calls Mary the "Mother of Jesus," it is Jesus who reveals and assigns her vocation to her when he

calls her "woman" and appoints her to be the mother of the beloved disciple while she is at the foot of the cross.

178. Two passages in John (2:1–5 and 19:25–27) describe Mary as mother in a basic way: at the beginning and end of the event at Cana and then at the foot of the cross. But the passages also emphasize the distance Jesus puts between his mother and himself, inasmuch as on both occasions he addresses her as "woman" and not as "mother." Is it that he is unwilling to think of Mary as the one who brought him into the world? No, the context shows rather that he wants to give Mary a role beyond that of simply physical motherhood.

179. At Cana Mary asks nothing of her Son but reveals a fact and then addresses the servants. The fact she points out is a deficiency that affects the festivities. It is Mary who makes known what is not going well. That is the way in which she intercedes with her Son. Here she already shows by her intervention how believers should listen to their fellow human beings and make known their needs so that Jesus may come to their aid.

180. The one confronted with this need is a Jesus whose mission is at this moment precariously balanced: his "hour has not yet come." Jesus is present at a human celebration not in order to satisfy needs felt there but to manifest his glory and inspire faith. It is this latter purpose that he makes known in advance by performing the sign.

It is in this way that the theological perspective of the gospel reveals itself. Mary is present at this revelation, although she does not yet realize it.

181. The troublesome question, "What concern is that to you and to me?" does not simply underscore the limitations of Mary, who does not immediately understand how and when the glory of Jesus will be revealed. It also invites her to adopt the outlook of her Son and to abandon her own initiative in order to follow his. It can be said that in this sense the episode of Cana is a milestone on the way of Mary's conversion, for she is made to understand that her role henceforth is to lead servants to her Son and to listen to his word and obey it fully.

182. Mary will experience for herself that obedience to a message and a call for renunciation are a source of blessing. Full of confidence, even before she knows what Jesus will do, she can say to the

servants: "Do whatever he tells you," thereby urging them to act with a faith as unheard of as her own.

183. The "discipleship" that is already found in the servants at the feast in Cana is found again in the person of the beloved disciple. Mary accepts and makes her own her relationship to the servant-disciples. She is present both in the family group and in the community of disciples. She submits to this twofold relationship and agrees to pass from the first to the second, but she will enter fully into this second relationship only after the crucifixion: There the Mother of Jesus will become mother of the disciple. The crucified Jesus calls upon her, his natural mother, to become mother of the disciples as represented by the beloved disciple who is so close to him in his passion and resurrection.

184. *The Gospel of John structures three elements: Mary-as-Mother-of-Jesus, Mary-as-woman, and Mary-as-mother-of-the-disciples, in a theological gradation: starting with Mary "Mother of Jesus," it proceeds by way of Mary as "woman" to Mary "mother of the disciples" with a new kind of motherhood that is of a different order than the first and that the church professes with him.*

MARY AND THE FAMILY OF JESUS

185. Without denying the bonds of blood or the physical motherhood of Mary, Jesus relativizes them and even refuses to see them as privileged in any way: his mother, his brothers, his sisters are those who do God's will (Luke 8:19–21 and parallels; Luke 11:27). Jesus henceforth sees his mother as a believer and a servant.

186. Those whom the Synoptic Gospels describe as the "brothers of Jesus" are likewise called upon to move beyond their direct understanding of him as a member of the family and open themselves to the revelation of his deeper identity. When Jesus is told that his mother and his brothers are outside looking for him, he answers that his mother and his brothers are in fact those "who hear the word of God and do it" (Luke 8:19–21 and parallels). There is here a break between Jesus and the familial group with which he is connected; there is even a painful break with his mother that suggests the sword which Simeon foretold (Luke 2:35) as piercing her soul. Of this same

family group John tells us that "not even his brothers believed in him" (John 7:5).

187. After the ascension, however, Mary and the brothers of Jesus will gather with the apostles in a shared adherence to the risen Christ (Acts 1:14). They become his brothers and sisters through faith and are then among the first in the multitudes of brothers and sisters whom Jesus wins for himself through his paschal mystery.

188. The faith journey of Mary and the journey of the brothers and sisters of Jesus to conversion are exemplary for believers. The latter are shown that their adherence to Christ cannot be without a rending at the very heart of their lives, until they are able in all truth to confess the man Jesus to be the only Son of God.

189. *Mary, who was so close to the human Jesus as his mother, had to experience the passion and death of her Son in order to become a disciple in the church. She thereby warns Christians that they cannot bypass the cross and resurrection in entering the community of their Lord.*

THIRD ARTICLE: MARY IN THE COMMUNION OF SAINTS

190. The third article of the Creed has to do with the Holy Spirit and the church. The church was born of God on Pentecost through the gift of the Spirit that was given to it. When the disciples were gathered in the upper room, waiting in prayer for this inaugural moment, Mary was present in the midst of the little Jerusalem community of some one hundred and twenty brethren (Acts 1:14–15).

The Communion of Saints

191. The communion of saints is grounded in its center, which is Christ Jesus under whose authority the church brings together the believers of every age who have been sanctified by his grace. It thus brings about the unity of his body on earth and in heaven, the militant church and the triumphant church, which are mysteriously united despite separation in time and place and the break that is death. For those who believe have already "passed from death to life" (see John

5:24; 1 John 3:14) or, in Pauline language, "neither death nor life...can separate them from the love of God" (Rom 8:38–39).

192. This communion of saints is experienced in the liturgy,[12] which transcends space and time and unites the celebration of the community on earth with the eternal praise of the heavenly community.[13] It is especially at the eucharistic memorial of Christ, at which the church gives thanks and praise to the Father in the Spirit, that the praying community links the memory of the saints of all times and places—of Abel, Abraham, and Melchizedek[14]—to the women and men who today are still witnesses and martyrs of their faith. In praise rather than in sadness these individuals celebrate their conformity "with the sufferings of Christ" (Phil 3:10–11) as they await the resurrection which the "first-born" among them has already experienced (Rom 8:29).

193. Our attentiveness to the liturgical dimension of the communion of saints brings us into agreement with the Orthodox Churches, for which the liturgy is the test of Marian piety. And in fact it is by way of icons and liturgical texts rather than of sermons, treatises, or dogmas that the spirit of Orthodox Marian theology is best grasped.

194. In the communion of saints we also remember, out of the anonymous throng which "no one could count" (Rev 7:9), those "athletes" of the faith (see 1 Cor 9:26) who are for us forerunners and models to be followed: the witnesses of the two Testaments, the martyrs and the confessors,[15] and among them the one closest to Jesus in the flesh, the Virgin Mary.

From the Undivided Church to the Confessional Churches

195. The granting to Mary of first place in the communion of saints was the result of a lengthy development. She did not enjoy this precedence in the very early church which confessed Christ as the source of all witnessing and the first of all the martyrs and which initially honored Stephen as the first one "to give back to Christ the blood which he shed for us."

196. The most significant text of the undivided church on the place of Mary in the communion of saints is certainly the Roman

Canon of the Mass, the central part of which was already known to Ambrose. At the head of all the saints being remembered this Canon places "glorious Mary, ever Virgin, Mother of our God and Lord Jesus Christ." That canon was the source of what would become the Western canon of the Mass.[16]

197. Before honoring Mary as the first in the communion of saints, the veneration of God's people for exemplary servants of this God had to be given to Christians who were not martyrs but "died in their beds," such men and women as Athanasius, Martin, Ambrose, Monica, Augustine, and Gregory the Great.

198. Mary thus found her place first of all as a virgin and prototype of consecrated virgins, and she did so thanks to the zeal of nuns, who were encouraged by bishops, especially Athanasius and Ambrose. It was after being head of this cortege, which she leads to Christ, that Mary became the foremost of all the saints.

199. This historical development makes sense only if Mary's precedence does not mean an exclusion. Other prayers, no less authentic than those of the Roman Church, can today use other, fully legitimate, precedences.

200. It is fitting to remark that outside the liturgy Catholics, too, practice a whole series of devotions that give a privileged place to other saints besides Mary. Though the popularity of these is perhaps excessive and too often based on legend, it is nonetheless an important sign that Mary does not eclipse the immense "cloud of witnesses," as can be seen from the devotion to Martin, Boniface, Patrick, Francis of Assisi, and so many others.

201. This popularity of the saints in Catholic devotion should not make us overlook the great comparable figures, members of the same great throng of witnesses (though this name is not used) in the churches that have sprung from the Reformation: John Huss and Marie Durand, Dietrich Bonhoeffer and Martin Luther King, and so on.

202. The Orthodox Churches, for their part, venerate such saints as Maria Scobtsova, starets Seraphim of Sarov, and Silouane, and canonize them. But this church also clearly asserts the preeminent place of Mary in the communion of saints. This unchallenged place belongs to her for the simple reason that she is an icon of the church and the mother of believers. She is the one who by definition is at the

head of those whom Christ declares "blessed" because they "hear the word of God and obey it" (Luke 11:28; see 8:21). Her preeminence shows clearly in the fact that she alone among human beings is called *Panagia,* "*all* holy" or "*most* holy."

CONCLUSION

203. As we made our way through the three articles of the Creed we have done so with Mary. We have accompanied her on her journey from the lowly young Jewish girl of Nazareth to her position of precedence in the communion of saints, which she acquired because she was the one God chose to be the mother of the Messiah.

In her Magnificat Mary sang of her unique destiny: she is the humble servant of the Lord for whom God—holy is his Name!—has done great things; she sees herself called "blessed" by all generations because she believed in the promises given to Abraham. As a result of her Yes to the angelic message, she would become the mother of her Lord. Though mother and blessed, Mary would not forget either her own origin or the greatness of him who was to take flesh in her, and was to transcend all the limitations of time and space as the "light of the nations" and the "glory of Israel."

PART II

Disputed Questions and the Conversion of the Churches

Preface for Part II

After this necessary dip into the history of the church and the testimony of the scriptures, we find our churches and our hearts painfully wrenched, as it were, when it comes to Mary, mother of the Lord and servant of God. When we ask with St. Paul, "Is Christ to be divided?" must we not acknowledge that as far as the Virgin Mary is concerned we are even more divided?

It is to this question, which is by no means the subject of a calm academic debate, that this second part of the Dombes Group document, *Mary in the Plan of God and in the Communion of Saints,* will endeavor to give answers. As it does so, it must not lose sight of the conversions demanded of all parties if they are to receive these answers as hopeful for the union of Christians and not as an admission of disagreement among the churches. This second part is, then, a direct continuation of the first part, which is a preliminary to it and an indispensable foundation. In fact, the first part, with its ecumenical reading of history and scripture, endeavored to analyze the lengthy story and basis for the "disputed questions" that are explored here at the doctrinal level (Chapter 3). As is customary in the Group's documents, this second part will end with proposals regarding the "conversion of the churches" (Chapter 4). Readers must have worked their way through the first part if they are to approach this second part with a full knowledge of the facts.

The primary purpose of a presentation is not to repeat point by point what the book itself will say, not even to put it in other words so that it may be better understood. Its purpose is rather to lay bare the secrets of hearts, as it were, by "filming" some sequences in the process that will surely end in this: that all the Christian Churches will together listen to Mary as she sings her Magnificat.

Can we speak of Mary as *cooperating* in salvation? Can we grant her a *perpetual virginity*? Not content with calling her the consecrated virgin par excellence and the first nun, are we to go still further? Must we turn her entire existence into a sinless journey from her conception to her assumption by her Son into the glory of the Father? Must we even derive from this theological "dream" the two dogmas proclaimed as articles of faith by the pope of Rome? Finally, are we to *pray to Mary*? How and to what extent?

The Principles at Work

In answering so many questions, the first principle we applied was that of justification by grace through faith, the principle that was foundational for the Churches of the Reformation, the Pauline principle by which "the church stands or falls" but which also makes it possible to judge every particular doctrine. It was in the light of this principle that in the course of lengthy debates among ourselves we analyzed, criticized, and finally understood the doctrine of Mary's "cooperation," but in the *very precise* sense that will be explained. The substantial agreement, which we think we have reached on this decisive issue, is linked to the basic truths of the faith, and undoubtedly represents the major advance which the Group is submitting for critical study by the faithful of the two traditions here in dialogue.

A second principle of a quite different kind has guided our thinking: the principle of the "hierarchy of truths," which was set down by Vatican Council II and accepted and taken over by a number of churches. This principle makes Marian theology, in the literal sense of this term, something that is not secondary indeed, but second in relation to Christ on whom it depends and from whom it receives its legitimacy. This being the case, are the differences that persist among us of such a nature as to prevent ecclesial communion? A corollary of this principle is that it is licit and even necessary to draw from the fundamental biblical datum the consequences for faith and piety that it implies and that do not contradict it. Here vigilance and felt need must always go together.

"Cooperation"

The term "cooperation" automatically brings confusion to the minds of many Protestants: this word with its "co-" suggests—wrongly, indeed—that Christ, the sole mediator, and his mother are associated as equals. Yet we cannot do without the word for lack of anything better. Moreover, it is a given by reason of its perennial use in Catholic documents. The Orthodox for their part speak of a *synergy*.

"Cooperation" (the quotation marks will always be used in our text) means that grace, which is always first and absolute, not only does not exclude a human response but on the contrary elicits and makes it possible and even obligatory. The active response of Mary in her fiat was part of her passive reception of the favor bestowed on her, the woman "filled with grace," that she should become the mother of the Lord, the *theotokos*, the Mother of God. The term "cooperation" in no way derogates from the conviction that the decisive, saving response is given solely and in its entirety by the only Son who takes flesh, gives himself up, and thereby effects salvation by himself, once for all, and for all human beings. But this salvation must be accepted. This receptivity is nothing else than renunciation of the self in order to let God act. A gift is certainly always the act of a giver, but the act is completed only once the gift is received by the one to whom and for whom it is given. The gift unites giver and recipient in an irreversible covenant. Grace that calls becomes grace that makes a response possible.

"Mary intervenes on behalf of the saved." No confusion can be allowed here. She is the first of believers; she gives the example of faith, which is not a doing but a receiving. For it pleased God to give himself in Christ in such a way that it becomes possible for human beings to respond to his love. This gift, in which the Son "strips and humbles himself," makes it possible for every human being to enter into this self-humbling and to imitate it by leaving it to God, the only sovereign, to effect this salvation and give "the will and the act" that belong to it. Creatures, delivered from sin, are able to praise God as Mary, who did not seek to be the mother of the Savior, does in her

Magnificat. It was to the divine election that Mary consented. The thanksgiving of the saved is a response to the sovereign grace of God. Protestants, who are unyielding on the principle of justification by grace alone, see the human response as part of the work of sanctification which glorifies God by a consecrated life.

The response also involves responsibility, an idea expressed by "cooperation" as understood in these pages. We must be watchful to bring it back to this understanding when it drifts away.

The fundamental agreement that we have been able to find among us is all the more important in that the point is an essential one, namely, the relationship between the sovereign grace of God and human freedom, between God's plan of salvation and the necessary response of its beneficiary. The solution proposed here leaves no doubt about the absolute character of God's elective grace; but it insists no less on the human response, which is an integral part of it as is attested by the mystery of the incarnation.

The Two Marian Dogmas

The two Marian dogmas likewise seem to go beyond what the biblical witness expressly justifies; above all, however, they risk separating Mary from the rest of mortals, of whom she is one. How are we to suppose that she lives body and soul in heaven? Even more, how are we to understand that she was "preserved from original sin"? The Protestant suspicion is that at this point and in a tangible way she has been made to move away from her status as creature and has been given a status parallel to that of her Son, who was born without sin and has ascended to heaven.

Moreover, the very fact of turning this twofold exception into dogma, and at such a late stage, inevitably makes Protestants very critical of them. Did a dogma have to be proclaimed in order for us to think that Mary, being completely saved by Christ, never experienced sin otherwise than as a music lover, listening to beautiful music, is suddenly distracted by a chandelier tinkling in the room? The music is perfect and the chandelier is outside it, and yet the listening is disturbed within by no fault of the one listening.

Following the path opened by this weak parable, would it not be unsuitable to get up, stamp one's feet, and cheer under pretext of cooperating with the music? On the contrary, does not "cooperation" mean living and acting in the interior conviction that Christ is the sole mediator? How, then, do the Catholics proceed?

With regard to the assumption, they acknowledge that this has been the common possession of the church since the sixth century, with Mary anticipating the common destiny of the faithful as a favor to the one who carried the Son of God within her body. She is not separated from him by death. Her holiness embraces the whole of her life and does not stop with her decease.

Moving, then, in the opposite direction, Catholics do not see why she who was one day to give life to the sinless one should not be fitted to make that act of consent and motherhood. If her holiness embraces her entire life, why should it not be hers from her very conception? Whence the idea, then the conviction, and finally the Catholic definition of her "Immaculate Conception." But this second Marian claim was in fact resisted for centuries, precisely in order to guarantee the humanity of Mary who, like every creature, had to be redeemed from original sin, since salvation by Christ is necessary for all without exception. The solution adopted was to understand the Immaculate Conception not as an exemption but as a "preservation" through a kind of anticipation of what the other redeemed would experience, each at his or her proper time.

The two claims, extensive though they are, are by no means intended to remove Mary from experience of the human condition. On the other hand, they do show in the person of Mary the success of God's plan for humanity as a whole, a success that is anticipated in her.

Without being obliged to accept the conclusions of the Catholic position, Protestants can acknowledge the uprightness of the intention at work, one which for their part they express while keeping strictly to the biblical testimony about the mother of the Savior and while taking seriously its immediate implications, as we saw in connection with "cooperation."

Is it not enough, then, to observe that our convergent interpretation of these dogmas does not imply that they must also be accepted by churches which were not parties in their promulgation?

This interpretation does assume, however, that in the spirit and intention that presided over the promulgation there was "nothing contrary to what the gospel says." No suspicion should immediately call into question either the purity of purpose on the Catholic side nor the reason for abstention on the Protestant side, since the intention on both sides is to emphasize the closeness of Mary to Jesus and her dependence on him. Watchfulness, mutual and fraternal, is the best insurance against both distortion and denial.

The Perpetual Virginity of Mary

"Perpetual virginity" seems to be a qualitative condition for what these dogmas proclaim, namely, that the holiness of Mary, which is her personal renunciation in the service of the Lord, permeates and shapes her entire life, turning it from a potential human undertaking into an irreversible commitment to God's plan of salvation—as well as a full and complete participation in the communion of saints, which makes all of us brothers and sisters in him who is "the first-born from the dead" among them (Rom 8:29).

Even though Protestants can defend a position that sees Mary as a married woman and mother of a family, like any other married woman, and takes literally the words about the brothers and sisters of Jesus, they can nonetheless accept and magnify the "virginity" of Mary in a spiritual and symbolic sense. Catholics can legitimately understand "brothers and sisters" to mean cousins, in keeping with the broad sense of those words in antiquity; they can therefore maintain, with the tradition, that the virginity which presides over the mystery of the nativity permeates the whole life of Mary, which was consecrated once and for all to the Lord and his service. Her fiat did not cease with her firstborn. These two positions, which are equally justifiable at the level of the reserved biblical witness, are not mutually exclusive, inasmuch as the quality expressed in virginity is a disposition of the heart which persists, whatever might be the hazards, if not the choices, of life. In these circumstances, are the divergent positions not compatible, since behind the explicit language used, the reasons given on each side spring from a shared conviction regarding the sovereign grace of God?

Marian Devotion

There remains the question of Marian devotion, the point at which veneration turns into invocation and invocation into prayer to Mary and the saints. The mother of God is *invoked* by the Orthodox Church and the Catholic Church, but she is already *evoked* by all the Churches on account of her presence in the Bible and in the creeds. Is the difference between veneration and invocation one that cannot be tolerated?

Here again, when Protestants are unable to address any prayer to Mary or the saints, Catholics can only agree inasmuch as, strictly speaking, no prayer or praise can be addressed to anyone but God alone and, more specifically, to the Father through the Son in the Spirit. Catholics have recourse to Mary and the saints only to ask that they intercede for them with God, not because such intercession is necessary or more efficacious, but simply in order to enter together with them into the great intercession that is as it were the constant expression of the solidarity among believers which even death cannot end. Intercession is thus the everlasting conversation of believers with their God in their concern for one another. It is within these limits that Catholics can legitimately turn to Mary and the saints, as they do in the Angelus or the rosary, in which they simply ask Mary to pray for them. Protestants who reject such prayer out of fear of confusion or excess must nonetheless be on guard not to forget to praise God for Mary and for the saints he has given them.

May we not humbly ask, not that those who invoke Mary should cease to do so nor that those who evoke her should invoke her, but rather that both should, in their understanding of the faith, be brotherly witnesses to the convictions of their brethren? These convictions would no longer be a cause of separation and an admission of differences within a unity "already given."

Conversion and Confession

If the gentlemen of Port Royal were still living, we would doubtless have the right to expect from them a treatise on the conversion needed for entering an ecumenical world. They would not be wrong to understand this commitment as a grace, especially when it consists in never believing in Christ without also maintaining the hope of achieving a unanimous view of Mary through him—unanimous without being uniform, for must we not recognize that even on this sensitive point the symphony of faith demands these kinds of dissonances? Unison would eliminate them. Disunion springs from disagreements; unity would harmonize the disagreements.

When the Dombes Group speaks as it does, its Catholic members do not "sell off" any of the truths which the Catholic Church requires its faithful to accept in faith. When we appeal to the "hierarchy" of truths that a council acknowledged, we do not do so in order to move from the council to a placatory spirit and from this to compromise and shady deals. We speak as we do in order to express our beliefs in terms that aim at being welcoming, not placative. Let us be sure of what is meant here: welcoming not to accommodating types but to people who are poor in spirit because God loves them. People, that is, who know that pride can explain either the rejection of a dogma or its acceptance and who humbly ask the Lord to convert them to his word.

To confess the faith before the world is not to confess it against some one. Denunciation of an error has meaning only if we want to make the mistaken person understand the truth he is trying to state while expressing himself badly. How, then, can we expel from the ecclesial brotherhood those who, while rejecting a cult of Mary, undoubtedly do wish to honor the mother of the Lord? When they feel within themselves a fear that their brothers and sisters in Christ are tending to turn Mary into a kind of goddess, they remind us that Christian worship means praying to God alone through his Son in the Spirit.

The differences are undoubtedly profound, but the real reason for them can be understood and experienced only on a shared journey and in a shared conversion of the Church of Christ, which we are.

That is what we have attempted in this volume, which contains the words "controversy and conversion" in its title. If another title had not already been taken, and if we could have used it again without pretentiousness or unsuitability, we could have said "confessions" instead. Yes, but "confessions" in the manner of Augustine, not indeed an outpouring of base actions but a confession of faults, such as is inseparable from the confession of faith and spurs us to the confession of praise. Such is the threefold confession that unites this book.

> *We confess, Lord, that we are guilty in regard to our common confession of the faith of the apostles when we err by excess or defect concerning the Virgin Mary, instead of joining in her confession of praise to the God who accomplishes in her and in us what to our minds is unthinkable and to our hearts impossible.*

Alain Blancy and Maurice Jourjon
Co-presidents of the Dombes Group

3

Disputed Questions

204. ◆ Using the three articles of the creed, we have stated what unites us in our confession of faith regarding Mary, the mother of the Lord. We must now turn to questions on which we have to admit there are differences. At the same time, recollection of the "hierarchy of truths"[1] allows us to give these questions the status they deserve, which is not secondary but is indeed second by comparison with the essentials that unite us. There are points of faith that are, without qualification, central; there are others that are more peripheral. This hierarchy provides a standard for determining the points that continue to separate us and those that do not.

205. In this determination, to which we shall now proceed, we will be inspired by a concern to answer the following questions: In Christian teaching about Mary, which elements form part of the needed unanimous acceptance of the Christian faith? On which elements can there be legitimate disagreement? Under what conditions and in what spirit can certain differences be accepted?[2]

206. Our differences have to do with four difficulties on which we shall try to speak with all possible clarity. Sometimes we shall be able to speak with one voice. Sometimes we shall have to fall back on two parallel statements.

These issues are:

—the "cooperation" of Mary in salvation;

—the perpetual virginity of Mary and the meaning to be assigned to "the brothers and sisters of Jesus" in the New Testament;

–the two dogmas defined by the Catholic Church: the Immaculate Conception and the Assumption;

–and, finally, prayer to Mary.

THE "COOPERATION" OF MARY IN SALVATION AND THE RELATIONSHIP BETWEEN GRACE AND FREEDOM

207. One of the major points of doctrinal disagreement between Protestants and Catholics regarding Mary is certainly the Catholic claim that she "cooperated" in the salvation of the human race. Such a conviction seems to undermine the major stand of the Reformation: justification by faith in Christ, the only Savior *(solus Christus)*, independently of works. The difficulty Protestants have with Mary at this point only illustrates a very fundamental problem.

The Protestant Conviction

208. In the Protestant mind, the word "cooperation" is suspected of conveying the idea if not of an equality, then at least of a collaboration of the same order in our salvation. It is, after all, a word that has "co-" as a prefix. Protestant theology and piety also see in the word an independent role for Mary, or even a rivalry between her and Christ. In a famous passage, Karl Barth strongly protested against Catholic "Mariology," which he accused of "heresy." The main point of his attack is the "cooperation" of Mary:

> Every attempt to make her person the object of special attention, to give her an independent role, even a relative one, in the history of salvation is an attack on the miracle of revelation. For in so doing one tends to make this miracle dependent not only on God but, in addition, on human beings and their receptivity. But in the New Testament the situation is exactly the opposite....The New Testament knows of no glory that "rebounds" on the graced and receptive human being....[3]

Later on, the same writer says:

> Because she is the servant of the Lord, Mary says the memorable words: "Let it be done...according to your word!" and it is as a woman with this mind that she becomes "the mother of the Lord" after v. 43. Due to this text it can certainly not be maintained that the *theotokos* [Mother of God] of the Council of Ephesus is not biblical. But is she the *mediatrix omnium gratiarum* [mediatrix of all graces]? The *coredemptrix* [coredeemer]? *Regina caeli* (Queen of heaven]? How is it possible to build so many ideas, which are flagrantly "too much," on the *fiat mihi* [be it done unto me] and the motherhood of Mary?[4]

209. So too, when Catholics constantly claim that Mary's answer "included both perfect cooperation with 'the grace of God that precedes and assists' and perfect openness to the action of the Holy Spirit,"[5] Protestants ask: "Is it the Yes of Mary that makes the incarnation possible, or is it the decree of divine grace that makes Mary's Yes possible?" On this key point two theologians state the Protestant response as follows:

> *Karl Barth:* No receptivity, no exchange, no transmission of power can be envisaged, even with the most careful reservations. For faith is precisely not an act of reciprocity but an act which consists in renouncing any reciprocity and acknowledging the sole Redeemer apart from whom there is no recourse. Revelation and reconciliation are irreversibly one-directional; they are indivisibly and exclusively the work of God.[6]
>
> *Jean Bosc:* The only active, salutary human obedience is that of Christ himself in his humanity. It is he who gives to God humanity's decisive response, just as he is also God's gift. It is certainly possible to speak a certain conformity of the faithful with Christ in this obedience. But how is it possible to suggest a cooperation, which is in itself already perfect and complete in Christ, on the side of both the human being and God? This idea of cooperation seems to be at the source of the undertaking to establish a parallel human work that complements the work of the Lord Jesus Christ, when in fact this human parallel is already contained in his own work.[7]

But in an earlier work Jean Bosc also asked this question: "Does this mean we must 'deny the necessity of works'? Not at all! But these are never anything but the fruit of a grace that is all-sufficient and the thankful response of human beings to the perfect gift given to them in Jesus Christ."[8]

The Catholic Conviction

210. It must be acknowledged, first of all, that when faced with this radical challenge many Catholic theologians have taken a dangerous path and contributed to an improper use of the terms coredemption and mediation in application to Mary. The very term "coredemption" is objectively flawed, because it suggests that Mary's role is of the same order as that of Christ. Vatican II consciously abandoned the term; it has not reappeared since then in official texts[9] and ought to be deliberately dropped.

211. The term "Mary mediatrix" has on its side the fact of a certain use of it in the Middle Ages. While Christ is the "sole mediator between God and men" (1 Tim 2:5) in the proper sense of the term, we can say that in a derived sense we are mediators for one another, "insofar as the one Mediator chooses to work through them [believers] as instruments or channels."[10] But because the title of mediatrix has in fact been used for Mary independently of this communion of saints in which we all have a mediatorial role, it has become freighted with a considerable misunderstanding.[11] This is why an ecumenical conviction asks Catholics to avoid the word and asks Protestants to bear in mind that when they find it in an official Catholic document, their brothers and sisters are not calling the sole mediation of Christ into question.

212. Yet the term "cooperation" is kept in such official Catholic texts as Chapter VIII of *Lumen Gentium* (no. 56), where the ecumenical intention is clear. The term expresses something dear to the Catholic tradition, in which it is understood that for a human creature to "cooperate" always means to "respond" in faith, hope, and charity. There is then no necessary opposition between "cooperation" in the Catholic sense thus explained and the "thankful response of human beings to the perfect gift" (Jean Bosc) that is asserted on the Protestant side. To the question asked above,[12] Catholics can, in the full awareness of faith, answer that the divine plan of salvation did indeed make Mary's Yes possible through grace and grant a place for

this free response. Catholic language has doubtless not yet managed to avoid all misunderstanding on this point.

213. When the Catholic Church speaks of a "cooperation" of Mary in salvation, it does not locate this "cooperation" alongside the initiative of the Savior and Redeemer. To use a simple but vivid image, it does not mean to say that Mary adds a percentage, however minimal, to the work of Christ. Our salvation is one hundred percent God's work through Christ in the Spirit. Mary is located on the side of the saved and intervenes in virtue of the grace which she, like all other believers, has received. Even if her salvation takes the form of a preservation from sin. Mary is "redeemed" by the same title as each one of us.

Toward a Reconciliation

214. Since the term "cooperation" is there and is alive in the mentalities of both sides, we cannot act as if it did not exist. Our effort will therefore be to both purify and "convert" it, to "reconstruct" it, as it were. Some day, perhaps, a different term will emerge from our dialogue, one that is more satisfactory to all concerned, because it will be free of all equivocations.

215. Mary's "cooperation" is the fruit of an initiative of the Father, who looks upon "the lowliness of his servant" (Luke 1:48). It is also the fruit of the "kenosis" of the Son, who "emptied himself...and humbled himself" (Phil 2:7-8) in order to make it possible for the human race to respond. Finally, it is the fruit of the action of the Spirit, who disposes Mary's heart to be obedient. That is what happens at the moment of her fiat. Mary's humility is the fruit of the Son's humility.

216. Mary, for her part, enters into the same movement: she is willing to renounce control of her own life. By doing so, she becomes the icon or image of every believer who renounces self-love and enters into a relationship with Christ. Christ, Luther writes, "provides for himself a glorious bride, without spot or wrinkle; he purifies her in the bath of his life-giving word, that is, through faith in his word, in his life, in his justice, and in his salvation."[13] The Reformer goes on to speak of all believers and then of the Virgin:

> He [a Christian] ought to think: "Although I am an unworthy and condemned man, my God has given me in Christ all the riches of righteousness and salvation without any merit on my part, out of pure, free mercy, so that from now on I need nothing except faith which believes that this is true....Through faith I have an abundance of all good things in Christ." Behold, from faith thus flow love and joy in the Lord, and from love a joyful, willing, and free mind that serves one's neighbor willingly....
>
> We have a pre-eminent example of such a faith in the blessed Virgin. As is written in Luke 2 [:22], she was purified according to the custom of all women, although she was not bound by that law and did not need to be purified....She was not justified by this work, but being righteous she did it freely and willingly. So also our works should be done, not that we may be justified by them, since, being justified beforehand by faith, we ought to do all things freely and joyfully for the sake of others.[14]

217. Mary was first chosen to be the mother of the Lord: the word "election" signifies an absolute divine priority. It was because Mary had been justified by grace alone and in faith, that she could be associated with God's work in Christ. Her "cooperation" was unique in regard to the nature of what she did, for she was the mother of Jesus and raised him. She "cooperated" in the unique and universal event of salvation. But from the point of view of structure or of her status, her "cooperation" was not different from that of every person justified by grace. It was in its entirety the fruit of the grace of God. Would Augustine not say later on: "When God crowns our merits, he is but crowning his own gifts"?[15] Freedom can then become a source of works that manifest the salvation being lived out in the communion of saints. In Catholic language, we would say that these works were wholly God's gift and that they were also wholly the doing of the graced freedom of the human person. We would not, then, be speaking of an action of Mary that was independent of that of Christ. Her "cooperation" is not added to the action of God and, since it is the fruit of these gifts, it in no way detracts from the sovereignty of Christ.[16]

218. Mary was also present at the cross. She did not cooperate in the unparalleled sacrifice which Christ alone offered. Ambrose reminds us that "Jesus needed no help in saving all of us."[17] Yet "Mary

faithfully preserved her union with her Son even to the cross, at the foot of which (surely part of the divine plan) she stood (see John 19:25), sharing deeply in the suffering of her only son and uniting her maternal heart with his sacrifice."[18] She responded with all the freedom her faith gave her by accepting the loss of her Son Jesus and welcoming the beloved disciple as a son.

219. Mary is an example of the lot of all the saved. Salvation consists in a relationship: there is no salvation if this relationship is not accepted, if it does not meet with a response of thanksgiving. Passivity in the presence of grace, faith's "letting itself be moved" by grace—these are the source of a new activity; receptivity turns into obedience.[19] Docility to the Holy Spirit becomes an active force. The passivity is never total; in a second moment receptivity itself becomes active. But every response is at one and the same time the work of God's grace and the work of human freedom stirred into action by grace. The only thing that belongs exclusively to human beings is the rejection of grace.

Alexander Vinet, a Protestant theologian, expressed all this in an admirable way in the nineteenth century:

> We do not say: "Work, *even though* God produces in you the will and the work"; rather, we say with the apostle: "Work, *because* God produces in you the will and the work" (Phil 2:12–13). It has been said that Christian wisdom is to be at rest as if God were doing everything, and to act as if he were doing nothing. Preferably, let us say that he does everything. He made us who act; he creates in us the will to do; he does through us everything that we do, but he does it through us and does not wish to do otherwise.[20]

220. But here a distinction is needed: acceptance is not a work. One who accepts a gift plays no part in the initiative that produces the gift. On the other hand, a gift is not fully a gift unless it is received. Strictly speaking, there is no gift unless the intended recipient accepts it; if he does not, there is only the offer of a gift. In a sense, the giver needs the recipient if there is to be a giving. A gift is a kind of appeal of the giver to the recipient. The response to the gift is part of the gift.

The gift of God which is Christ himself is subject to this law of free acceptance: "How often have I desired to gather your children together as a hen gathers her brood, and you were not willing!" (Matt 23:37). Augustine would say later on: "He who made you without you will not save you without you."[21]

221. These thoughts fit perfectly with the Pauline logic of justification by faith and of the faith that works through love (Gal 5:6). In the Gospels Jesus does not hesitate to say: "Your faith has saved you" (Matt 9:22; Mark 5:34; 10:52; Luke 7:50; 8:48; 17:19), thereby attributing to faith that which is the work of grace. We ought never fall victim, then, to a logic of rivalry, for that which is acknowledged as God's does not in any sense do away with the human being; what is given to the human being is not taken away from God. What is true of the faith of every believer is true of the faith of Abraham and the faith of Mary.

222. Such is the paradox of the covenant: it is unilateral on God's part and becomes bilateral to be effective. The covenant exists before the response, and its rejection in no way thwarts the plan of God. The Yes to it was said before us by God and by Christ "When Christ came into the world, he said: 'Sacrifices and oblations you have not desired, but a body you have prepared for me....Then I said, ..."See, God, I have come to do your will"'" (Heb 10:5–7, citing Ps 40:7–9 LXX). On the other hand, it is important that we in turn say a full Yes. Christianity rejects the idea of a God who is solitary. God causes human beings to exist, and human beings cause God to be the God of the covenant. God willed to give his Christ an existence in the flesh through the fiat of Mary.

223. It is advisable to distinguish also between the element of "cooperation" that plays a part in the unique, dazzling moment of justification and the element that affects the ensuing life of the justified person.

In a first phase, the acceptance of justification is a "response." But in a second phase, which the Protestant tradition prefers to call the phase of sanctification, a new possibility is given to the justified person. Paul speaks of us as heirs of God and coheirs with Christ, and grace is a beauty that shines out in all the actions of the children of God (see 2 Cor 3:18).

224. The word *response* calls to mind the word *responsibility*. Because Christ wills to save us as a single body living in communion and solidarity, he gives us the power to help one another on our journey toward the kingdom. This power is an element in the priesthood of all the baptized, which makes us, through participation in the mystery of Christ, prophets, priests, and kings (see 1 Pet 2:9). Since that is what we are, grace enables us to share in the redemption which Christ alone brings. Those who live in Christ are able to "cooperate" in the salvation of the world through the response of their entire life, their intercession, their sufferings offered in love, and all the works done in faith.[22] The often misunderstood words in Colossians 1:24 express a "cooperation" that in no way calls into question the uniqueness of Christ's redemptive act: "In my flesh I am completing what is lacking in Christ's afflictions for the sake of his body, that is, the church." As Luther says, we can become Christ's for others.[23]

225. An example of the new "cooperation" made possible by the grace of justification is the cooperation of ministers. By his words Paul built up the church: he cooperated. He did so, however, beginning with the Yes which he uttered in faith and which was made possible by the Spirit. He dared to say of himself and his companions: "We are the cooperators *(synergoi)* of God" (1 Cor 3:8; literal). This "cooperation" describes the action of the servants of the Master, who alone is the "operator." Based on this scriptural foundation, the term "synergy" is traditional in the East.

226. The "cooperation" of Mary is likewise a service for the carrying out of salvation. It is set apart by its object, since in her situation the Virgin played a unique role, in grace and through faith, chiefly at the birth and death of Jesus. Mary cooperated through her response of faith, like every justified person, through her obedience, her motherhood, and all her actions as "servant," one of these being her intervention at Cana.

227. This debate over Mary undoubtedly leads us back to a much more comprehensive debate, as K. Barth saw very clearly, namely, over the consequences in the human person of justification through faith and over the ability of human beings to "cooperate," through grace and faith, in their salvation. This is the same problem that arises with regard to the "cooperation" of the church.[24]

Therefore,[25] while the viewpoint on reconciliation that is taken here has to do primarily with the role of Mary in the economy of salvation, we think that it has a much wider application and can advance our dialogue in the church.[26]

THE PERPETUAL VIRGINITY OF MARY AND THE REFERENCES TO THE BROTHERS AND SISTERS OF JESUS IN THE GOSPELS

228. The existence of brothers and sisters of Jesus is a datum of the New Testament. The difficulty in interpreting the fact does not in any way impinge on our common faith in Christ, the first-born of the Virgin.[27]

229. The question which modern readers spontaneously ask when they read of these brothers and sisters is not the question of the editors of the New Testament. The latter, especially the evangelists, emphasize the point that the way in which Jesus understood and carried out his ministry was at least surprising to his family, who had not followed him along the roads of Palestine and who joined the group of his disciples only at the end, after his death and resurrection. All this highlights the unique and unparalleled insight Jesus had into a ministry to which no one in his family urged him.

230. In light of recent discussions of the subject,[28] it is impossible from the viewpoints of history and exegesis to prove with certainty that the brothers and sisters of Jesus were such in the strict sense of the terms or, on the other hand, that the references were to a family in the broader sense that included cousins.[29] The various references are not textually decisive, although the mention of four brothers of Jesus (Mark 6:3) would make a modern reader think spontaneously of four blood brothers. We must admit that the texts of the New Testament do not provide us with the evidence needed to answer such a question. The arguments heaped up on both sides are based on assumptions that are easily turned on their head.

231. The surprise, not to say the scandal, felt by some Christians, Catholic and Orthodox, when one accepts that Jesus had brothers and sisters in the proper sense of the terms, is due to their faith in

the perpetual virginity of Mary. The acceptance is an attack on their Mariology, not on their Christology. For, according to a conviction dear to both Orthodoxy and Roman Catholicism, if Jesus looked beyond the family group with which he clashed (Matt 12:46–50; Mark 3:31–35; Luke 8:19–21), and made all of us his brothers and sisters, then "sound thinking about Mary" (Origen[30]) requires her to have renounced all carnal relations in order to remain the mother solely of her Son Jesus.

232. The churches springing from the Reformation take note of this outlook, even though it is not scriptural. The Reformers understood the term "brothers" *(adelphoi)* in the sense of cousins and in a nuanced way preached the perpetual virginity of Mary.[31] Some minority Protestant currents have always asserted this perpetual virginity and have tried to interpret it as a special consecration of Mary as a woman, a mother, and a figure of the Church.[32]

On the other hand, exegetical inquiry has led many Protestants to the contrary position. Still others think that a sure affirmation of faith cannot be based on an uncertain scriptural attestation.

233. Catholics think that what is said in scripture does not in any way contradict the claim of perpetual virginity for Mary, and they therefore accept the conviction of faith that arose in the early church on this subject. Some Protestants, for their part, while regarding the biblical testimony as insufficient for grounding a matter of faith, also think that the assertion of Mary's perpetual virginity can have a spiritual sense that is not to be brushed aside. In any case, the distinction between historical evidence and the conviction of faith must be respected.[33]

THE CATHOLIC DOGMAS OF THE IMMACULATE CONCEPTION AND THE ASSUMPTION

234. We are aware in our approach to these two Catholic dogmas that all the Protestant confessions reject them and that the Orthodox think they have been defined and specified in an illegitimate manner within the setting of the doctrinal options available to the West. The Roman Catholic Church, for its part, has solemnly incorporated them into the content of its faith.

The first step in clarification is, it seems to us, to explain the two dogmas in a way that will make their meaning and intention intelligible even to those who do not accept them and that will let us know whether or not they contradict the shared fundamental confession of faith which we expounded in the first part of the present document.

Difficulties Common to the Two Dogmas[34]

235. The dogmas of the Immaculate Conception and the Assumption of the Virgin Mary are recent (1854 and 1950). They were intended to translate into doctrine the understanding of Mary that had developed through the centuries in the church's prayer and liturgy, namely, that she, the Mother of God, is "all holy" and that this holiness, understood in a global way and initially without being defined, was entirely at the service of the history of salvation and earned her the privilege of being associated, at the end of her life, with the glory of her Son.

236. As a result of this transition from a faith expressed in piety and praise to solemnly defined dogmas, these two claims about Mary constitute today one of the subjects of ecumenical disagreement. Their content, their formulas, and their foundation give rise to serious debates.

237. Many Orthodox have serious reservations about the two dogmas.

In their view, the Catholic dogma of the Immaculate Conception has no support in scripture and is overly dependent on Western tradition and the Augustinian interpretation of original sin, which differs from that of the East. They regard this dogma as resting on a juridical vision of redemption, according to which Mary benefited in advance from the future merits of Jesus Christ. While the Orthodox hail Mary as "all pure" and "wholly spotless," this is not because of her conception but because it was granted her not to let herself be controlled by sinful nature. They maintain that even after the fall creatures can with divine help fulfill their vocation of being "images of God," and it is in this sense that they see Mary as the most perfect fruit of humanity.[35]

238. As for Mary's final lot, the Orthodox tradition speaks more often of her "dormition," even if it does also use the word

"assumption"; the two ideas are not coextensive.[36] It confesses that without ceasing to belong to our human race and because she had received the privilege of giving bodily birth to the Word of God, Mary reached the highest degree of holiness a human being can achieve. It confesses also that she was the first to benefit fully from the grace that her Son won for us by his passion and resurrection.

239. The Orthodox also reject the two dogmas as promulgated by the Catholic Church. That is, the doctrines were defined without any external circumstance making such a definition necessary, and they were proclaimed after the separation of the churches, apart from any council, and by popes who drew upon their authority as infallible teachers. We may think, however, that the Orthodox accept to some extent the substance of these dogmas, especially that of the Assumption.[37]

240. The Christians of the Reformation appeal above all to the fact that these two dogmas have no explicit biblical basis. As a result, the dialogue between Catholics and Protestants is here marked, in a concentrated form, by the whole classic disagreement on the normative character of biblical testimony, on the reading and understanding of scripture within the living tradition of the Church, on the "sense of the faith" of the faithful (which in this instance finds expression primarily in piety), the intervention of the magisterium, and the "reception" of magisterial definitions.

241. The Reformation Churches have thus raised objections more fundamental than those of Orthodoxy in regard to the doctrines of the Assumption and the Immaculate Conception. These objections do not arise solely because these two teachings have led in the Catholic Church to dogmatic definitions. They are also to be explained by the ambiguous forms of devotion that may have accompanied the celebration of the Marian feasts. They are due, in addition, to properly theological difficulties which ecumenical dialogue has had to take into account. Protestants recognize fully the holiness of Mary in the communion of saints, but they do not think that they must on that account, starting with faith in Christ, go so far as to affirm the Immaculate Conception and the Assumption. Furthermore, they think that due to the uncertainty that surrounds them these questions call for a great deal of reserve, which has not always been respected.

242. In this area, the ecumenical dialogue will be an opportunity for Catholics to put to work the principle of the "hierarchy of truths," as formulated by Vatican II.[38] In the name of this principle, they will have to acknowledge that the doctrines of the Immaculate Conception and Assumption, while certainly not secondary, are second in importance to the central nucleus of the Christian faith. Granted this, we see what the issues are in the dialogue between Catholics and Protestants. On the one hand, it will be necessary to find out what these two affirmations say that is important about Christ and about human beings who are saved in Jesus Christ. On the other hand, it will be necessary to define clearly the points on which disagreements still exist between us, while distinguishing between differences that separate and differences that prove compatible with ecclesial communion.

243. The dialogue must in any case determine if and to what extent the dogmas of the Immaculate Conception and the Assumption represent not "novelties," as the Protestants used to say, but interpretations of a datum of the Christian faith that has its ultimate basis in the testimony of scripture–interpretations, then, which are at the very least legitimate and must find their proper place in the "hierarchy of truths."

Historical Reminders[39]

244. The two Marian dogmas were defined at the end of a lengthy history in which popular piety, liturgical prayer, and theological reflection were closely intermingled. Theological reflection may have preceded in some instances, but most often it accompanied (sometimes in a critical way) or even followed the progression of religious affectivity and devotion that led to the proclamations of 1854 and 1950. The point we are making is the importance, for a proper understanding of such dogmas, of the ways that led to the Marian definitions and of the historical context in which the definitions were promulgated.

FROM THE AFFIRMATION OF MARY'S HOLINESS TO THE CATHOLIC DEFINITION OF HER IMMACULATE CONCEPTION

245. The development that led to the definition of 1854 was marked, in the West, by a number of theological controversies. In the East, the affirmation of Mary's holiness in the early centuries did not

preclude the occasional acknowledgment that she had some faults (for example, her difficulty in believing the angel at the Annunciation, her untimely intervention at Cana, or even her presence at the cross[40]). In the West, on the other hand, beginning with Ambrose, her holiness was the object of claims that increasingly refused to admit any shadow of fault. Moreover, this acknowledgment of Mary's perfect holiness was lastingly marked in the West by the debates over original sin. These debates were often due to the views of Pelagius (ca. 360–ca. 422), for whom Mary's perfect holiness is the model of what human nature can be when it rejects sin, and to the views of Julian of Eclanum (ca. 380–ca. 445), who thought that the fact of Mary's holiness was a reason for denying original sin. These views were combated by Augustine, whose position, though awkward in its presentation,[41] was clear in its substance. While accepting that the fullness of personal holiness was granted to Mary as Mother of God, he nevertheless refused to accept that she, unlike other human beings, was conceived without sin. She too benefited by the grace of rebirth.

246. Western reflection on the holiness of Mary continued to be controlled by this position of Augustine and marked by doctrinal disquisitions on the nature and effects of original sin. This reflection led in the Middle Ages to a clash of views on how to understand the conception of Mary, the celebration of which originated in the East but spread throughout the West beginning in the twelfth century. Some rejected the immaculate conception of Mary on grounds of the universality of original sin.[42] Others, such as Bonaventure and, above all, Duns Scotus, asserted the immaculate conception of Mary and provided the formulation of it that would make its way into Western theology: Mary was redeemed by Christ by being "preserved" from original sin in anticipation of the merits of her Son.

247. While a movement in favor of the immaculate conception began in the fourteenth century, the debate among theologians remained a lively one and led the magisterium to intervene when representatives of the strict Augustinian line of thought challenged the legitimacy of veneration paid to the Immaculate Conception and of preaching and teaching on the subject.

248. In 1483 Pope Sixtus IV pronounced that there was to be freedom in regard to this point of doctrine and that neither side was

to call the other heretical.[43] The Council of Trent referred to this statement at the end of its own Decree on Original Sin, where it said that it did not intend to include "the blessed and immaculate Virgin Mary, Mother of God" in the decree.[44] Thus even while affirming the universality of original sin, it set aside the case of Mary, for it recognized the validity of the argument that sought to reconcile the universality of original sin and redemption with the immaculate conception of Mary, but without settling the basic question.

249. As the controversies continued, we see successive popes intervening—while they forbid each side to anathematize the other, they move increasingly in the direction of seeing Mary as preserved from original sin, even while not imposing this doctrine. In particular, this was the burden of the letter of Alexander VII (1661) from which the definition of 1854 would borrow some formulations.[45]

250. A quick review of history thus makes it clear that while piety and fervor constantly pushed in the direction of celebrating this "privilege" of Mary, the core of the theological resistance to the doctrine of the Immaculate Conception—this across all the confessions—was always the fear that by exempting Mary from original sin one would be casting doubt on the universal necessity of salvation through Christ. This resistance compelled theologians in favor of the doctrine to develop formulations that, while asserting Mary's privilege, would keep her subject to the necessity of being saved by Christ.

251. The definition of the Immaculate Conception by Pius IX in 1854 had for its context the revival of Marian devotion in the nineteenth century. The definition was preceded by a consultation of the worldwide episcopate, a large majority of which proved to be in favor of the definition (546 in favor, 57 against). The document consisted essentially of the formulations which theological reflection had developed.

THE ASSUMPTION OF MARY

252. The historical development that led to the definition of the Assumption of the Virgin Mary was not marked by controversies as important as those connected with the Immaculate Conception. Moreover, this new definition was intended simply as a solemn confirmation of a devotion that already existed and had hardly been debated in either East or West.

253. The question of Mary's final lot began to be raised in the wake of the Councils of Ephesus (431) and Chalcedon (451), inasmuch as the proclamation of the *theotokos* called attention to Mary's body. Thus the idea of the glorification of this body developed. In the sixth century the feast of the "memory" of Mary (like those in "memory" of the martyrs and saints) became the feast of the "Dormition" of Mary. This word did not deny the reality of Mary's death but it did suggest a death of a special kind; but there was as yet no question of an assumption of Mary body and soul.

254. Beginning in the eighth century, Byzantine homilies on the Dormition began to assert the Assumption in the proper sense along with the death of Mary. Although these homilies could appeal to the imagery of the suddenly numerous apocryphal stories that fed popular piety, the arguments developed in them were theological in substance: the body that had carried and given birth virginally to the incorruptible Word of God could not have experienced the corruption associated with bodily death.

255. The West had no difficulty in taking over the theological motifs developed in the East, as well as the feast of the Dormition of Mary, which would later become the feast of the Assumption. The only debate in which the Middle Ages engaged had to do with the authority of two apocryphal works: one, attributed to Jerome,[46] which regarded the bodily assumption of Mary as too bold an idea to be held as a truth of faith; the other, attributed to Augustine,[47] which without reference to the legends justified the bodily assumption on theoretical grounds. It was the latter approach that would win the day. Later discussions dealt only with the kind of certitude with which the Assumption of Mary could be affirmed and believed.

256. The only magisterial document on the Assumption of Mary is that of Pius XII in 1950. It emerged from a historical context that was marked by a growing development of Marian piety, the building up of a "Marian movement," and the establishment of a new branch of theology known as "Mariology."[48]

257. Like Pius IX before him, Pius XII consulted the episcopate on the "definability" of the doctrine of the Assumption and on the opportuneness of such a definition. This consultation yielded an "almost unanimous" response.[49] Some bishops did express doubts

about the opportuneness of a definition, especially for ecumenical reasons. The solemn definition was issued at the end of the 1950 Holy Year.

Theological Thoughts on the Assumption

258. If we look first at the dogma of the Assumption (even though it was promulgated after that of the Immaculate Conception), the reason is not simply that it raises fewer difficulties for ecumenical dialogue. It is also because certain views on the final destiny of Mary spread more quickly that those having to do with the initial phase of her life.

THE TERMS OF THE PROBLEM

259. The first difficulty the Reformation Churches have with this dogma is that it is not attested in the scriptures. Another difficulty of Protestants is that the Assumption is often understood as a gift exclusive to Mary, thereby seeming to separate her from the condition common to all human beings. Finally, it seems odd that a teaching belonging to faith was not promulgated before the twentieth century.

260. On the Catholic side, difficulties with the dogma often arise from mistaken ideas that can affect the very understanding of the dogma. Thus the Assumption of Mary may be confused with the Ascension, which refers to Christ alone. Above all, it risks being linked to the belief that the Virgin did not experience death; but this is not by any means part of the definition of the dogma. When poorly understood, the doctrine of the Assumption keeps alive a disincarnate vision of Mary as though she did not fully share the condition of humanity.[50]

261. It is one thing to accept a dogma; it is another to understand its anthropological and theological meaning. With an eye on the latter, we shall offer some thoughts that *describe* this meaning. While conscious of the difficulties involved, we, both Catholics and Protestants, think it necessary before all else to study the dogma of the Assumption in the light of the resurrection of Christ. The resurrection is due unqualifiedly to an initiative of God who by rescuing

his Son from the tomb made him the firstborn from among the dead. When seen in this light, the Assumption means that Mary, not due to any personal merit but in virtue of divine grace, already experiences the final lot of those who belong to Christ and have been raised up in him.

TOWARD A BETTER UNDERSTANDING OF THE ASSUMPTION

262. It is important to remind ourselves here that "resurrection," in the biblical sense, is not to be thought of as the reanimation of a corpse, nor as the immortality of a soul stripped of any relation to a body, nor as a form of reincarnation in another life that is still subject to the limitations of space and time. It is rather the "resurrection of the flesh," as the Apostles' Creed puts it. "Flesh" here signifies the person in its unity and integrity, that is, its "spirit," its "soul," and its "body," this last being understood here not as physical components destined to perish, but as a dimension that does not cease to be closely linked to the identity of the human person. For the new life for which Christians hope belongs not to their souls alone but to their entire person, which has necessarily been influenced by its bodily life in the world: by the way it has behaved there, and by the events of its history or, in short, by everything that has allowed this person to become what it is. "Just as the story of a life is written in the wrinkles of an elderly face, so the human subject unfailingly preserves the history of the world that was 'its own.'"[51] The "flesh" that rises is therefore everything that carries the mark of the way in which a human being has related to himself, to the world, to others, and to God.

263. It is that kind of "resurrection" that the Christian faith attributes to Jesus, and this resurrection becomes the basis of our own hope: "Since we believe that Jesus died and rose again, even so, through Jesus, God will bring with him those who have died" (1 Thess 4:14). The Assumption means that this hope is already fulfilled in Mary and that God has bestowed the "resurrection of the flesh" on her by raising her "body and soul, to the glory of heaven." God has thus granted her the very thing of which the resurrection of Christ was promise and pledge for every believer.[52]

264. Mary's lot was by no means dissociated from that which Christian tradition very soon acknowledged as proper to the martyrs

and, more broadly, to the saints, whom the tradition sometimes describes as "other Christ(s)." It is also significant that the Catholic dogma of the Assumption was proclaimed on the feast of All Saints; what it says of Mary must be situated within the realm of the communion of saints, of that "cloud of witnesses" who have gone on before present-day believers as they follow after Christ (Heb 12:1), of that "assembly of the firstborn who are enrolled in heaven" (Heb 12:23). If the Assumption is explicitly attributed only to Mary—because as Mother of God she was in an exceptional position—it nonetheless signifies the achievement of a salvation which is not reserved to her alone but which God wishes to bestow on all believers.

265. Thus understood, the dogma of the Assumption speaks to us of our own future; it marks out the object of the hope that fills us even now in historical time, for "the creation waits with eager longing for the revealing of the children of God," and "we ourselves, who have the first fruits of the Spirit, groan inwardly while we wait for adoption, the redemption of our bodies" (Rom 8:19 and 23). The Assumption tells us that God has already anticipated, for the Mother of his Son, the salvation for which Christians hope.

Theological Thoughts on the Immaculate Conception

266. The end refers back to the beginning; thus the final lot of Mary bids us reflect on the first phase of her existence and therefore to inquire into the dogma of the Immaculate Conception. In the dialogue between Catholics and Protestants this dogma undoubtedly raises more difficulties than does the dogma of the Assumption. The obstacles arise not only from the lateness of its promulgation or from the controversies that have accompanied discussion of the Immaculate Conception from the nineteenth century to our own day; there are also specifically theological difficulties that are connected with different understandings of the relationship between the Creator and his creatures, of original sin, grace and freedom, and the place of Mary in the economy of salvation. We shall proceed by first clarifying the terms of the problem, then singling out those elements of a consensus which we can establish in the future, and finally by defining the differences which have thus far not been surmounted.

THE TERMS OF THE PROBLEM

267. Protestants understand, of course, that the dogma of the Immaculate Conception is connected with the doctrine of the Incarnation, in the sense that according to Catholics the coming of the Son presupposes that his human mother was preserved from every sin, and this from her own very conception. But it is precisely this presupposition that is a difficulty. Protestants object that it contradicts the Gospel revelation according to which God came to visit sinners: human creatures are not graced because they are lovable, they are lovable because they are graced. From the Protestant point of view, the doctrine of the Incarnation does not at all imply that Mary was preserved from sin from the very beginning. This preservation was not necessary if Mary was to say her fiat; on the contrary, it is necessary to hold that even as Mother of the Savior she bore the mark of original sin. The objection, therefore, is not only that, according to Protestants, the dogma of the Immaculate Conception is not attested in the scriptures but also that its basic motivation seems to contradict biblical revelation.

268. Catholics, for their part, insist on reminding us that the doctrine of the Immaculate Conception does not cast doubt on the fact that Mary shared the condition of every creature who is called to salvation; on the contrary, we must understand that Mary was herself "redeemed" by having been preserved from original sin.[53] But Catholics assert that she benefited from this favor "from the moment of her conception," and it is on this point that they differ from Protestants. At the same time, they acknowledge that different motives led to the definition of the dogma: sometimes the proponents emphasized the point that the body of Jesus could not have been born of flesh marked by sin; sometimes they understood the Immaculate Conception as the mark of holiness that was granted to Mary in a completely unmerited way, made her a woman "filled with grace" (see Luke 1:28), and so enabled her to utter the fiat of the Annunciation. This second reason is in itself more satisfying and is more promising in the perspective of dialogue with Protestants. Just as the Assumption of Mary signifies the completion of the salvation which God grants to all human beings (see nos. 264–65), so her Immaculate Conception signifies her vocation to the holiness to which God calls everyone (see Eph 1:4).

ELEMENTS OF A CONSENSUS

269. With the contending positions thus clarified, we are able to bring out several points on which there can henceforth be a consensus between our two traditions, even if one of the two does not approve the dogma as such.

We see, first of all, that in fact our different churches share the same concern to respect unreservedly the sovereignty of Christ, both by bearing in mind that Mary herself (like every creature) needed to be saved by her Son and by stressing the fact that the Immaculate Conception is to be understood only in relation to the mystery of the Incarnation.

270. Secondly, the positions of both of our churches are based on a theology of grace. If it be true that the Protestant Reformation legitimately emphasized the unqualified initiative of God in the gift of his grace *(sola gratia)*, then the Catholic doctrine of the Immaculate Conception must likewise be understood in the light of *sola gratia*. The reason: the Immaculate Conception is not due to the personal merits of Mary, but is entirely the work of God who "chose us in Christ before the foundation of the world to be holy and blameless before him in love" (Eph 1:4) and who preserved Mary from all sin from the moment of her conception in order to prepare her to become some day the Mother of his Son.

271. Even if Protestants and Catholics do not agree on confessing that Mary was exempted from all sin, both do agree on saying that she lived out the human condition, which is one of progress, discovery, heartbreaks, weaknesses, and limitations, If Jesus himself experienced temptation, nothing allows us to exclude Mary from that same situation, Her holiness was not given to her once for all and complete. The scenes of the loss of Jesus in the temple ("His parents...did not understand": Luke 2:50) and of Mary intervening in the public life of Jesus are evidences of this road she had to travel.

272. Finally, dialogue on the Immaculate Conception can only profit from progress in ecumenical reflection on the subject of "cooperation." On the one hand, to the extent to which Catholics admit that Mary's fiat at the Annunciation was possible only by the grace of God, they can rightly present the Immaculate Conception as a radical expression of the grace through which it pleased God, from the very

beginning, to make it possible for Mary to agree to the Lord's plan. And to the extent to which Protestants recognize that the gift of grace did not dispense Mary from responding freely and actively to the will of God, they can better understand the meaning of the Catholic position that the Immaculate Conception did not remove Mary from the human condition but rather prepared her to be able some day to give an active response to God's initiative, just as every other redeemed creature does.

REMAINING DISAGREEMENTS

273. The points of agreement, which we have just brought out, will also help us, by contrast, in particularizing the disagreements that remain between us on the Immaculate Conception. While our two traditions care equally about honoring the incomparable holiness of Christ and the absolute primacy of divine grace, they do not draw the same conclusions from these principles and do not look in the same way at Mary's situation within humanity as a whole.

From the viewpoint of the Reformation Churches, God's gift to Mary certainly precedes the moment of her fiat, but it is not necessary, theologically, to move backward from that point and to assert a holiness granted to Mary from the moment of her conception. In addition to not being founded on scripture, this claim does not do full justice to a correct understanding of divine grace and of Christ's work. For how could Mary have been touched by grace if she had not first had experience of sin? How could she have been preserved from sin "from the moment of her conception" when, according to the revelation in the Gospel, Christ came to call and save sinners? And how can we conceive that Mary was able to benefit by anticipation from a salvation wrought one day in the future by her Son? The doctrine of the Immaculate Conception always runs the risk of detaching Mary from the common human condition, because according to this teaching, she is the only creature to have been preserved, from the very beginning, from original sin.

274. The Catholic doctrine of the Immaculate Conception maintains that redemptive grace reached Mary at the very first instant of her existence. Although the doctrine is not formally attested in the scriptures, it is to be understood in the light of God's plan in the

history of salvation; that is, in order that Mary might be truly able to utter her fiat at the Annunciation, God willed that she be rescued from the very outset from the curse of original sin. We must therefore not imagine a time in which Mary lived in a sinful condition before benefiting from grace; we must say, rather, that even though she belonged completely to our human race, she was preserved from all sin from the very first instant, and this by pure grace, because she was called to become some day the Mother of the Savior. In this sense, too, she was "filled with grace." This perspective does not imply that Mary's holiness is to be confused with that of Christ, who is the sole redeemer of the human race. The doctrine of the Immaculate Conception means rather that this holiness of Christ was granted in advance to the woman who would one day carry him in her body; in other words, Mary was holy from the very first moment only because she benefited by anticipation from the holiness communicated by her Son.[54] Far from removing her from the human condition, the holiness thus bestowed on her was what restored to her her true humanity, by making her capable of one day accepting the message of the angel and thereby making possible the carrying out of the divine plan. Looking at the Immaculate Conception in this light, we see how it, no less than the Assumption, speaks in fact of our own calling: if Mary was "filled with grace" in a unique way, it was in order to bear witness to the fact that we in our turn are touched by the superabundant gift of grace that God has bestowed on us in his beloved Son (see Eph 1:6).[55] This vision transcends all logical necessity; it belongs to the realm of divine excess.

CONCLUSION

275. Our ecumenical discussion of the Assumption and the Immaculate Conception should make it possible to move beyond the controversies inherited from the past and better understand our respective positions on each of the two Marian claims. It has led us to recognize elements of agreement between our traditions and, above all, to bring out more clearly the differences that remain between us.

Catholics accept the dogmas of which we have been speaking, and they place them within the "hierarchy of truths" according to their relationship with the center of the Christian faith. Protestants, on the other hand, think that these dogmas do not help in the attainment of a better understanding of the essentials of the faith, and that they often give rise to a devotion which has no direct connection with the Gospel.

At the same time, however, we recognize that these differences do not undermine our communion in one and the same faith in Christ. In fact, we are all convinced that the claims concerning the life of the Virgin from its beginning to its end must always be ordered to our understanding of the person of Christ and of the salvation Christ has brought to us.[56]

INVOCATION OF MARY AND THE SAINTS

276. Another point of disagreement has to do with the "cult *(cultus)* of Mary," the importance of which in the piety of the faithful and in pastoral care should not be underestimated. The ambiguity of the phrase is due to the vague sense given to the word *cultus.* The seventh ecumenical council (Nicea II, in 787) clearly distinguished between the legitimate veneration *(doulia)* of images (icons) of the saints, and adoration *(latria),* which may not be given to them because it is reserved to God alone. Strictly speaking, there can be worship or "cult" only of God, Father, Son, and Holy Spirit. The fundamental path taken by Christian cultus or worship runs to the Father through the Son in the Holy Spirit. The addressee of worship is always God. There is no more direct way than the Son of God for reaching the Father.

277. This is why according to ancient tradition, and speaking strictly, we do not pray to Mary or the saints, because prayer, which is a form of adoration and an act of *latria,* can be addressed to God alone. But a broad use of the word "prayer," although theologically incorrect, has led to speaking of "prayer to Mary" and the saints.

Above and beyond this common practice, disagreement remains between Catholics and Protestants on the idea of prayer to Mary understood as prayer through Mary, that is, a request to Mary that she intercede with God for us.

278. The first form of invocation is praise freely offered to God for the grace bestowed on Mary. This praise is not limited to believers

on earth, the "saints" of Paul's letters; it includes the entire church in heaven and on earth, as we read in a preface of the Protestant eucharistic liturgy, in which the Father is thanked: "In communion with the universal Church, with the angels and all the host of heaven, and in a shared joy, we extol and magnify your glorious name: Holy, Holy, Holy...." This kind of invocation is a manifestation and expression of a communion which death cannot break, even if it changes the manner of the communion. It has its place in the trinitarian movement of praise of the Father, through the Son, and in the Spirit who intercedes in us, for us, and through us (see Rom 8:26).

279. Praise of Mary, in response to the invitation in the Magnificat: "All generations will call me blessed" (Luke 1:48), is to be found in the great Reformers, especially in Luther, Zwingli, and Bullinger, and with greater reserve in Calvin. But Luther himself reacted vigorously against the excesses and distortions in the Marian veneration of his time. He even says: "I would like to get rid completely of veneration of Mary because of the way it is abused."[57]

280. The term "veneration" can include honor and praise, especially such as are meant, suggested, authorized, and even urged by the biblical passages on the Annunciation and the Visitation. Such veneration means praising God with and for Mary, hailing the work of God in her, and thanking God for her exemplary response.

281. It is in this framework that the question must be raised of the legitimacy of a prayer of intercession that is addressed to Mary and the saints. According to Catholics, such a prayer can only be one that is passed on to God, who alone can answer it and grant it as he pleases. It is not separated or separable from any other prayer, but is united to the prayer of the saints of all times and places, living or dead, in Christ. In the communion of saints prayer, and especially the prayer of intercession, implies no separation between those who pray, those for whom they pray, and him to whom this prayer is addressed. Intercession is an expression of communion. It is the unending conversation that goes on within this communion.

282. The Reformers, for their part, reject every request for intercession that is addressed to Mary, since it would presuppose that she has a role as an effective instrument in the economy of salvation or that she "cooperates." Zwingli says that we have only one intercessor,

and Bullinger adds: only one mediator. Calvin rejects the idea that Mary is a "treasurer of graces."[58] This attitude is connected with a general refusal to venerate the saints.

283. Catholics, for their part, willingly acknowledge that Marian devotion has often given rise to excesses in the outward forms of piety, in books of Marian spirituality, and in the vocabulary used in theological and pastoral formulations. These excesses did not end with the great abuses of the sixteenth century, but have always accompanied the Marian movement in one or other fashion.[59] They may have led people to think that in the Catholic faith Mary is considered, for practical purposes, to be a real goddess. While the Catholic magisterium has never professed such excesses, it has not combated them with the needed clarity.

284. The Catholic faithful ask Mary and the saints to "pray for us"; in other words, they invoke them in order to ask their intercession. This is expressed in the second half of the Hail Mary, the part that is of ecclesiastical origin: "Holy Mary, Mother of God, pray for us." It is repeated endlessly in the litanies of the saints. This is the veneration known in theology as *doulia*. For in the final analysis, the honor given to the saints and the intercessions addressed to them reach God, the author of all grace.

285. The Second Vatican Council gave specific new guidelines for the cult of the Virgin Mary. It reminds Catholics that this cult "differs essentially from the cult of adoration, which is offered equally to the Incarnate Word and to the Father and the Holy Spirit: (*LG* 66). It asks theologians and preachers "to be careful to refrain as much from all false exaggeration as from too summary an attitude in considering the special dignity of the Mother of God" (*LG* 67) and to protect the Christological orientation of this cult.

286. Protestants and Catholics agree that we must, with the scriptures, *venerate,* that is, love, respect, and honor the Virgin Mary and praise God for her whom "all generations" are bound to called "blessed."

They also agree in saying that we ought to *imitate* her and regard her as an example, especially by uniting ourselves with her prayer and praise of the Father.

They disagree on the subject of *invoking* her: the Protestant tradition does not allow her any intercessory role, whereas Catholics entrust themselves to her maternal intercession and say to her every day: "Pray for us sinners."

287. Must we stop short at this statement of facts? Be content with this opposition? Cannot veneration include for Protestants the angel's words in the Hail Mary or the words of a sister, such as "Blessed are you among women," both drawn solely from the scriptures?

On the other hand, can intercession be thought of as other than an integral element in the communion of saints in heaven and on earth, of human beings and the trinitarian God—an intercession that is united with the eternal intercession of the Son with the Father, and is matched by the intercession of the Spirit within those who are sinners and justified? Far from being an indication of distance and difference, is it not rather the sign of a communion and a sharing? Far from being private or exclusive, does it not rather open us to the world God so loved and to the entire creation, responsibility for which rests with those who have been chosen to serve before his face, beginning with the Mother of the Savior, the blessed Virgin Mary? Prayer to and through Mary will thus be a prayer like and with that of Mary. It will not erase distinctions, but neither will it become a cause of separation.

If this were the case, would not the contradiction and incompatibility between the Catholic and Protestant positions tend to diminish, while theological and pastoral vigilance would prevent both excess and narrowness? Then different types of piety could live side by side, without suspicion or obligation, and not be the cause and effect of division.[60]

288. God's plan of having humanity, which is created in his image and likeness, achieve a communion in his Son led him to place Mary at the very heart of this plan of salvation. Persuaded as we are of this, we have together come up with the following convictions:

We reject as an insult both to Mary and her Son any attempt that in the name of "cooperation" would limit the absolute sovereignty of grace.

Without dwelling at excessive length on the question of the brothers and sisters of Mary's firstborn, we prefer, like her, to listen to her only Son with his countless brothers and sisters, in order that we may receive the salvation that is her Son, as she did before us and did better than us.

We are unable to accept that the same faith does not unite both those who profess that this salvation took hold of Mary (from the first moment of her existence on to the glory of heaven) and those who stand hesitant before these dogmatic devotions which they do not find in the scriptures. We are therefore resolved to advance together on our journey in the communion of saints. For it is in fact an identical faith in Jesus that bids us not be separated because of her who was not a source of our confessional divisions.

This is why, in keeping with the thrust of our method, we wish now to offer our churches some suggestions about conversion; we offer them not as a conceited message from above, but because we need their support if we are to submit to the obedience of faith.

4

Toward the Conversion of the Churches

289. Our historical review has shown that the division between us appeared at the moment when Mary was isolated from both Christ and the communion of saints and when devotion to her took on exaggerated forms. On the Catholic side, then, "Mariology" was unduly separated from Christology and ecclesiology. This is why the decision of Vatican II to make its text on Mary a part of the Constitution on the Church was an act of great importance for our ecumenical reconciliation. This ecclesiology made it possible to make Mary a part once again of the people of God. On the Protestant side, there is an acknowledgment that a proper confession of Christ requires something to be said of Mary, and this in the name of the incarnation itself.

290. The proposals we have formulated for our respective churches have for their purpose to bring us closer to one another by giving Mary the place that belongs to her in the Christian faith—her full place, of course, but also nothing but her place.

A CATHOLIC CONVERSION

A Conversion of Attitude

291. Catholics cannot fail to be aware of the judgment, often still a very stern one, that is passed by Protestant theologians in the ecumenical movement on the place of Mary in their church. Thus,

Reformed theologian J. Moltmann writes: "The discrepancy between Church teaching and the New Testament is nowhere as great as in Mariology."[1] And in the article on Mary in the recent *Encylopédie du protestantisme* A. Birmelé writes: "Roman dogmas call into question the reference to Scripture alone, Christ alone, and grace alone. The conviction that this is so is confirmed by the development of popular devotion and the multiplication of Marian pilgrimages."[2] More generally, the Protestant mind remains alienated from Catholic devotion to Mary. Even though there is no question of requiring that spiritual sensitivities find the same expression, this Protestant outlook demands of Catholics a justification and deeper study of their practice.

292. It is a historical fact that the person of Mary has played a key part in the popular religion spread by Christian evangelization. She has a threefold role:

–closeness: she is the mother who is attentive to all of her children;
–defense of cultural identity: she is celebrated as possessing the traits of each people;
–protection and healing: she is supposed to set people free of all oppressions and all illnesses.

Theological and pastoral discernment must be on guard against scorning the faith of the humble, even while evangelizing it in a way that keeps a mother goddess from hiding behind the traits of Mary and keeps the faithful from thinking that an affective relationship with Mary contains the whole of Christianity and the whole of the church. In like manner, the appeal to the sense of faith of the faithful *(sensus fidelium)* must be used with caution, for what is taken as such may spring from religious feeling rather than from the Christian faith.

293. In regard to our subject "Mary and the communion of saints" we must be attentive to the "ecumenical tradition" that is in process of formation. At the congresses which the Pontifical International Marian Academy has organized since the council, the ecumenical dimension is always present.[3] Another point to be stressed is the exceptional quality of the dialogue on Mary between Catholics and Lutherans in the United States.[4] We note also that many bilateral dialogues, as for example the one between Catholics and Orthodox, have

not yet found a place in our dossier, since they have not judged the subject to have priority.

294. Catholic theologians, too, have a great responsibility for the way in which the role of Mary in the Christian faith is explained. It is very desirable that they dispense with any "Mariology" understood as an isolated chapter of theology and focused exclusively on the person of Mary and, instead, return to an authentic "theology of Mary" that is integrated into the "mystery of Christ and the church." Although the majority of theologians did take this second approach after the Second Vatican Council, books are still appearing today whose content is objectively unacceptable. To take but one example: While it is legitimate to study further the connection between Mary and the Holy Spirit, it is impossible to set up a relationship between her and the Spirit that can be compared with the union of humanity and divinity in Jesus.[5] As part of the same shift in approach, the many Marian journals now in existence should pursue the task of purification already begun in their presentation of teaching about Mary and devotion to her.

A Doctrinal Conversion

"COOPERATION" OR THE ACTIVE RESPONSE OF MARY

295. *It seems to us that the doctrinal clarification which we jointly offered earlier on the subject of Mary's "cooperation" has produced a result which is adequate for expressing a communion of faith, even though it has not settled the entire problem in its various applications.*

THE TWO RECENT CATHOLIC DOGMAS

296. In the area of dogma, the proclamation of the dogmas of the Immaculate Conception and the Assumption are a matter that concerns only the Roman Church which formulated them. To the extent that this church regards itself as committed by its own declarations on the "hierarchy of truths," it ought to recognize that these two dogmas cannot oblige other Christians, since they were not part of the common expression of the faith at the times of separation.[6]

In point of fact, the assertion of the "hierarchy of truths" at Vatican II makes it no longer permissible to maintain some earlier claims in an unnuanced form.[7] The faith is, of course, always the same insofar as it is a response to the authority of God as he reveals himself. But, even apart from the historical and human dimensions of their transmission, some claims are so central that they attach to the very creed; others are subordinated to them. The statements of the faith form a complex whole in which a hierarchy exists and real developments can be discerned.

297. The Catholic Church of today cannot think of the Orthodox and the Protestants as being like Catholics who oppose its definitions and to whom it must issue serious warnings.[8] It should cultivate toward these Christian brothers and sisters the same attitudes of prudence and charity that it showed down the long centuries of theological debates on this question. What was a problem not of faith but of theological opinion in the church for nineteen centuries should not be regarded in the twentieth as something that separates us. Let us not forget that such a spiritual teacher as St. Bernard and such a master of theology as St. Thomas Aquinas retain their entire authority in the Catholic Church and have always been regarded as witnesses to a complete faith even after the definition of 1854, even though in their time they came out against the Immaculate Conception. And let us not forget that in 1661, in his Brief *Sollicitudo,* Pope Alexander VIII forbade the partisans and enemies of the Immaculate Conception to attack and anathematize each other. Should that not be the attitude of Catholics toward the Orthodox and the Protestants? If full communion were reestablished between the churches, a new dialogue on these subjects would then be necessary.

298. Would not the wisest thing be to agree on the following?

The Catholic Church would not make the acceptance of these two dogmas a condition for full communion among the churches. It would ask only the partners with whom it would renew this communion to respect the content of these dogmas and not to judge them contrary to the Gospel or to the faith, but to regard them as free and legitimate conclusions flowing from reflection by the Catholic consciousness on the faith and its internal coherence.

299. The recent example of confessions of Christological belief that were signed by the pope, and the patriarchs of ancient churches

long known as "non-Chalcedonian," shows that the most authoritative expressions formulated by councils can give rise to a true agreement on the faith by moving beyond old language that had become the subject of barren controversies.[9] It ought to be possible to do the same, again with a view to the recovery of unity, with the papal definitions of the Immaculate Conception and the Assumption.

300. In preparation for such a reconciliation, should not the Catholic Church pay heed to the reservations of the other churches and Christian confessions and try to offer a catechesis of these two dogmas that is more attentive to the witness of the scriptures? This catechesis ought then to serve as instruction in the faith for popular piety.[10]

THE PERPETUAL VIRGINITY OF MARY

301. Can the same principle of a "hierarchy of truths" be similarly invoked in regard to the perpetual virginity of Mary? Very much so, if we consider its relation "to the foundation of the Christian" faith and to a clear and solid attestation in the scriptures. The faith of our Protestant brothers and sisters in the divinity of Jesus Christ "who was conceived by the Holy Spirit and born of the Virgin Mary" remains the essential point. Nevertheless, we are dealing here with a conviction of faith in the early church, a conviction expressed in all its liturgies, which give Mary the title "ever Virgin," unanimously accepted by the local churches before the break in the sixteenth century, and accepted also by the first Reformers.[11] This tradition prevents us from simply applying to this difficulty the same principles of solution that we have applied to the two "modern" Catholic dogmas.

302. *The question, then, is whether or not the fact that many Protestants do not accept the perpetual virginity of Mary is an obstacle to membership in the same baptismal and eucharistic church. Although we are inclined to say it is not, we acknowledge that there must be a further and more thoroughgoing interconfessional dialogue on the subject.*

A Conversion in Marian Devotion

303. The difficulty in a Catholic conversion in this area is due to the fact that authentic Catholic teaching should have avoided the excesses of Marian devotion but did not. Vatican Council II presented

this devotion as a fruit of faith, and not the other way around: "Let the faithful remember...that true devotion consists neither in sterile or transitory affection, nor in a certain vain credulity, but proceeds from true faith, by which we are led to recognize the excellence of the Mother of God, and we are moved to a filial love towards our mother and to an imitation of her virtues" (*LG* 67).

DIRECTIONS TO BE TAKEN

304. Some years after the council Paul VI decided to reflect further, in an apostolic exhortation, on the place that Mary has in the public worship of the church and in the private devotion of the faithful.[12] In that setting, in which he already sketched out a way of conversion for the Catholic people, he urged them to a more discerning practice of Marian devotion.

305. The Christological element in Marian devotion must take first place: "There is...one mediator between God and humankind, Christ Jesus, himself human" (1 Tim 2:5). "In the Virgin Mary everything is relative to Christ and dependent on him" (no.25). Mary's relationship to the person and work of the Holy Spirit highlights the necessary ecclesial dimension of Marian devotion, because the Virgin is the first of the redeemed, the first Christian. The Virgin Mary's ties to God who is Father, Son, and Spirit, and her place in the Church are thereby located within the economy of salvation.

306. We shall make our own the four directions that Marian devotion needs to take according to Paul VI:

–*biblical:* Marian devotion ought to focus on the basic themes of the Christian message;

–*liturgical:* devotional practices should be in harmony with the liturgy while at the same time not being confused with it;

–*ecumenical:* devotion to the Mother of God should have "an ecumenical aspect...shown in the Catholic desire that, without in any way detracting from the unique character of this devotion, every care should be taken to avoid any exaggeration which could mislead other Christian brethren about the true doctrine of the Catholic Church. Similarly, the Church desires that any manifestation of cult which is opposed to correct Catholic practice should be eliminated" (no. 32);

—*anthropological:* Mary is a model not in her manner of life, which today is outdated, but in her courageous faith and active love: "Mary of Nazareth, while completely devoted to the will of God, was far from being a timidly submissive woman or one whose piety was repellent to others; on the contrary, she was a woman who did not hesitate to proclaim that God vindicates the humble and the oppressed, and removes the powerful people of this world from their privileged positions (see Luke 1:51–53)" (no. 37).

PRAYERS

307. The recitation of the Angelus and the rosary should conform to these norms:

The Angelus[13] derives its value from its simple structure, its biblical character, its historical origin that was connected with the call for keeping the peace, its almost liturgical rhythm, and its openness to the paschal mystery.

The rosary ("crown of roses") or chaplet is a form of litanic praise and invocation that focuses on the redemptive incarnation of Christ. It is a way of contemplating the life of the Lord.[14] Just as there are one hundred and fifty psalms, so there are one hundred and fifty Hail Marys. The rosary derives its existence from the liturgy and ought to lead back to it. There is, however, a "substantial difference" (no. 48) between the liturgy and the recitation of the rosary.

APPARITIONS

308. What are we to say of apparitions of Mary, such as those at Lourdes or Fatima? It is noteworthy that Paul VI's apostolic exhortation does not say even a word about them. Psychologists describe them as individual, nonpathological experiences that the eyes of faith interpret as experiences of a presence. The Catholic Church regards them as "private revelations,"[15] that cannot be compared with the revelation set down in scripture. They are not part of the faith; that is, each Catholic is free to assess them for himself or herself.

309. The official attitude of the Catholic Church to them has always been marked by the utmost prudence. St. John of the Cross asks us to "resist" special revelations as dangerous temptations.[16] In the eighteenth century Pope Benedict XIV set down a course of conduct

from which his successors have not departed: "The approval which the Church gives to a private revelation is simply a permission given, after careful examination, to make this revelation known for the instruction and edification of the faithful. One may refuse assent...to such revelations, even when approved by the Church...provided one does so for good reasons and without any spirit of contempt."[17]

310. The ecclesial magisterium has approved a cult at the place of such apparitions only in a minority of cases and after taking all the time needed for the clarification of the phenomenon. It applies two norms for discernment to them: the conformity of the message heard to that of the scriptures and to the faith of the church, and the spiritual fruits of conversion that appear on the occasion of pilgrimages.

311. Apparitions have for their purpose not to ground the faith but to serve it. They add nothing to the one revelation, but can be a humble reminder of it. They are sensible signs in which God communicates himself according to the capacities of those who receive them. They can be likened to an icon that, according to Eastern theology, is a "real objectification, inspired by the Holy Spirit...that generates and is the vehicle of presence."[18] They belong to the order of charisms, that is, gifts of God to a member of the body for the good of the whole body. Like all the exceptional charisms, they ought not to be sought but accepted with thanksgiving, discernment, and prudence.

312. Often, however, the spontaneous devotion of the faithful goes beyond this prudence and leads to a sometimes unhealthy curiosity regarding the most recent sites of apparitions and the extraordinary manifestations that take place there; it is as if their faith needed an indispensable confirmation. A process of pastoral instruction needs to be undertaken, as indeed it already has been at some sites of older apparitions, the purpose being to direct pilgrims toward an authentic conversion that helps them move from credulity to a faith in the message of Christ.

PREACHING AND CATECHESIS

313. It is not enough to acknowledge the exaggerations and deviations of the still recent past. It is also necessary to eliminate abuses of language in theological and pastoral discourse, as well as excesses in popular devotion and practice. It would be desirable, for

example, that the texts of hymns to Mary be corrected wherever they use "inflated"[19] formulas that attribute to Mary what is proper to God (for example, forgiveness). Should not statuary limit itself henceforth to the representation of the Virgin with her Son? Some local practices need to be subjected to sound criticism that may lead even to their abandonment.

314. There is an insistent need which preaching may not overlook. Preaching should never lead to veneration of Mary that is in bad taste or exaggerated. This veneration must always be faithful to the principle set down by St. Irenaeus: a proper understanding of Christ will necessarily bring Mary into the picture. If evocation becomes invocation (as in fact it does), the latter must never depart from the rule of faith *(regula fidei)*. Just as there is but one faith that makes one baptism necessary, so there is but one Lord who demands an attitude of devotion to his mother.

A PROTESTANT CONVERSION

A Conversion of Attitude

315. The process of conversion for Protestants should take place on two levels. First, they must acknowledge that a brother or sister in Jesus Christ can have devotion to Mary without thereby breaking the communion of faith. Second, the question is not whether the one party has too much devotion and the other not enough (which implies a false symmetry), but what it is on both sides that stands between the believer and Jesus Christ. Protestants need to ask themselves whether their too frequent silences about Mary are not prejudicial to their relationship with Jesus Christ.[20]

316. If we look at our respective traditions and join together in probing the scriptures to see the place of Mary in the history of salvation (as we did in the first part of this volume), our work will have concrete consequences for us. It is not a question simply of restraining Marian inflation in Catholic piety and restoring Mary to her place in Protestant piety (a little less there, a little more here!). A good deal more is at issue in ecumenism. There is need of a new look

at the differences that remain between us, especially when it comes to the dogmatization of Mary's place in the work of salvation.

Such is the form which the effort of conversion required of Protestants needs to take.

317. In treating of Mary we must get away from the world of sterile controversy and the facile caricatures which each side readily attributes to the other in order to dissociate itself from the other. In reacting to the overly large place of Mary in Catholic piety, Protestants are reduced to a silence that not only does not respect the Roman Catholic faith but also leads to a kind of self-censure that does not do justice either to the position of the Reformers or to Mary's place in the history of salvation.

318. For this reason we must greet some Protestant voices, and by no means the least outstanding, that have already called upon us "to look to the positive attitude which we, as children of the Reformation, ought to have toward the place of the Mother of the Savior in the things of which we Christians are certain." The author goes on to say that "a teaching on Mary is not only possible but necessary in Protestant faith and theology. Without this teaching, the critique of Roman Catholicism is distorted and certainly ineffective. In any case, we need only recall and recommend, in this respect, Luther's fine commentary on the Magnificat."[21]

Independently, then, of any possible deviation in Marian devotion, Protestants are urged to move out of their prudent reserve and restore Mary's true place in the understanding of the faith and in the prayer of the church.

319. This revaluation or rehabilitation of Mary and the unique place she occupies in the plan of God is not the fruit of an "ecumenical compromise" that would bring together quite different points of view, but a return to the Mary of the Gospels and the mark of a greater fidelity to the scriptures. Even Karl Barth, who was so strict in his criticism of Marian devotion, said explicitly about Mary: "There is one here who is greater than Abraham, greater than David, and greater than John the Baptist, greater than Paul and greater than the entire Christian Church; we are dealing here with the history of the Mother of the Lord, the Mother of God himself. This is a unique and unparalleled event."[22]

320. This Protestant vigilance should also lead us not to exaggerate the importance of Mary's place in the life of the Catholic Church. Her place in Catholic piety varies greatly, and the Sunday liturgy is very reserved in regard to her. The Marian dogmas and other statements about Mary are to be located within the "hierarchy of truths," and they do not occupy first place in Catholic teaching as a whole. Protestants are being urged to a new outlook that does not exaggerate: when they speak of the Catholic Church they must not confuse the center or essentials in the expression of faith with the periphery.

A DOCTRINAL CONVERSION

321. Everything has been recapitulated in Christ, and there is no longer an empty space that needs filling between God and us, between heaven and earth, between the present time and the future last time. Moreover, by our faith we are inserted into the long chain of believers: the apostles, prophets, martyrs, and witnesses of every age who have gone before us and who make up the communion of saints. Despite her special place as mother of Christ, Mary cannot be isolated from that communion, and this ought to be our first and truest veneration of her.

322. The proper place which we can restore to Mary exists only in the communion of saints, the predecessors and models of those who, with and after them, take their place in the "retinue" of the victorious Christ (Eph 4:8; Col 2:15). By their life and witness Mary and all the others share in one and the same communion of saints in Christ.

The "Cooperation" or Active Response of Mary

323. A careful rereading of the scriptures will lead to a salutary challenge to our understanding of Mary's role and place. While grace is always first, it also calls on each occasion for a response, the response of love to love. From this point of view, Mary is given to us as the decisive and perfect example of the Yes which Christian faith must utter. In this perspective, Mary can be regarded as model for the

believer who is justified by faith and not by works. As such, Mary, the "greatly favored one," the humble servant of the Lord on whom the Lord has looked with favor and who is therefore blessed among all women and is declared blessed because she has believed–this Mary is indeed a "model for the Church,"[23] for the people of God who are still on earth and advancing toward the kingdom; she is our sister:

> Mary, our younger sister, "the little girl," and by that very fact the elder sister of us human beings.
>
> Mary, the face of simplicity that has been so often distorted and stained–doubtless by one and the same action.
>
> Mary, the "blessed one," whose gaze pierced the heart of the angel and whose voice sang the Magnificat for us.
>
> Mary of Nazareth, graced and gracious, whose faith is a wonderful feat.
>
> A story, the focus of her own history, that speaks to us of the God of heaven made flesh in her.
>
> Mary, who was better able than anyone else to speak of this history.
>
> Mary, more than our mother; forever "Mary, our sister."[24]

324. Provided that all ambiguity is removed in regard to salvation being effected by the grace of Christ alone, Protestants could find a meaning in this "cooperation." Following the Reformers, they might see in Mary, the Mother of the Lord, the person who simply by her active response "cooperated" in salvation and thereby showed in an exemplary way how every Christian is sanctified. For, as "model of the Church" and within the communion of saints, Mary becomes "our mother and we become her children. Such is the overflowing goodness and consolation of God that he offers humanity such a treasure, by making Mary its true mother, Christ its brother, and God its Father."[25] "Cooperation," then, can be understood as that "imitation" of Mary to which Calvin calls all Christians.[26]

THE TWO RECENT CATHOLIC DOGMAS

325. A. Piepkorn, a Lutheran theologian, had this to say: "Regarding the maturation of some Roman Catholic ecclesiological insights that have found their first and seminal expression in Lumen Gentium and Unitatis Redintegratio: the day may come when it will be

admitted and acknowledged that the *entire* Church was not consulted before 1854 and before 1850, that the *entire* Church did not agree with these definitions or consent to them, and that, whatever be their degree of canoncial validity for those who accept the authority of the bishop of Rome, they remain open to question for the Church *as a whole.*"[27]

At that period such a viewpoint was still thought by its author to be a solution unacceptable to Roman Catholics. Thirty years of ecumenical dialogue have shown that the understanding of this difficulty has greatly increased, as can be seen from the message of conversion set before the Catholic side.[28] This new situation contains an appeal to the Protestant side and allows us to take the following position.

326. While the Protestants in the Dombes Group cannot accept the Immaculate Conception and the Assumption of Mary as belonging to the faith of the church, especially because these dogmas are not attested in the scriptures, they are nevertheless sensitive to their symbolic value and are willing to have their Catholic brothers regard them as dogmas of faith. If account is taken of what we have said about cooperation and justification by faith alone,[29] we are able to state that the interpretation of these dogmas no longer contains anything contrary to the proclamation of the Gospel. *In this sense, these dogmas do not create a difference that separates. For their part, the Protestants of the Group believe that it is quite possible to envisage a return to full communion in which each side would be free to respect the positions of the other side.*

THE PERPETUAL VIRGINITY OF MARY

327. With regard to Mary's title "ever Virgin," Protestants respect this as a statement that belonged to our common faith before the separation and now is part of the faith of the majority of their Christian brothers and sisters. *Whatever the difficulties with the claim, they do not fail to look upon Mary as the virgin par excellence, a title that will always be hers by reason of the virginal conception of Jesus.*

Mary in Christian Prayer and Praise

328. The respect due to Mary, which already has its place in the Protestant tradition, will never turn into adoration: "To God alone the glory!"

There are undoubtedly differences of degree in the veneration of Mary, and in this perspective Protestants will readily understand that other Christian traditions may go farther than they do in expressions of this veneration, but they will not accept a difference of kind between the veneration of Mary and the veneration paid to other saints or great witnesses of the faith. But on the Protestant side, what is the character of the "honor due to the holy and blessed Virgin Mary"?[30]

329. Moving beyond their silences, their theological controversies, and their watchfulness against the mariolatrous deviations that still exist, Protestants still need to restore to Mary a proper place, both doctrinal and liturgical, in the mystery of salvation and the communion of the saints. By so doing, they will make a useful contribution to the quest for communion among our churches and will better situate themselves within the great tradition of the entire church.

330. This implies that our Protestant Churches will give a proper place in Sunday worship and the Eucharistic Prayer to all these witnesses, especially in the major seasons of the liturgical year, such as Advent and Christmas, the passion and Pentecost, and will restore meaning to the feast of all believers (All Saints).

331. Through this effort at rereading the scriptures and this renewed understanding, our Protestant Churches will renew contact with their own traditions and, like some of the Reformers, rediscover the joy associated with the Marian feasts such as the Annunciation, the Visitation, and the Presentation in the Temple, all of which are directly connected with the mystery of Christ.

332. Finally, attentiveness to possible excesses of Marian devotion compels Protestants to question their own manner of praying, its limits and deficiencies. Does the sometimes excessive restraint of their liturgies leave room, within the communion of saints, for an authentic piety that does not succumb to sentimentality or unbridled enthusiasm? Attention to the truth of our way of praying is an exercise in conversion that all of us need.

333. "What is to hinder" (see Luke 18:16; Acts 8:36) Protestants from:

–singing joyfully and in faith of the place which the creed assigns to Mary?

—emphasizing the uncommon lot of the daughter of Israel who became the mother of Christ and a member of the church?

—bearing witness to the conversion of Mary, who added to her status as mother the more humble status of sister and servant?

—agreeing that the Magnificat sings in an exemplary way of their own faith and hope?

—being able to praise God still for what he allowed Mary to be and do, and not scorning those who for love of their Lord bring the name of his mother into their thanksgiving, using the very words of the angel at the Annunciation and of the blessing spoken by her cousin at the Visitation, and even the words of the elderly Simeon at the Presentation?

—seeing to it that this Gospel acclamation is always a proclamation of the mystery of the incarnation and salvation; that nothing is attributed to Mary the "mother" which belongs properly to her Son; but also that nothing is denied Mary in the communion of saints?

—remembering that Mary is at the beginning and end of the earthly ministry of Jesus, a witness to its start at Cana and its completion on the cross?

Conclusion and Summary

334. ♦ At the end of our journey must we still speak of "disagreement" between Protestants and Catholics on the subject of Mary? It is advisable to give a nuanced answer to this question.

Points of disagreement do remain, and we have studied them at too great an extent to forget them in writing our conclusion. But our concern in dealing with them has been to rid them of various "misunderstandings" that still burden them even today and to lessen their influence by striving always to make the compatibility of viewpoints as clear as possible. We have investigated at length whether and to what extent these disagreements are so serious that they touch the "foundation" of our faith.

335. We may therefore offer this conclusion: *As members of the Dombes Group, and in light of the proposals for conversion with which our journey ended, we no longer consider the described differences such as to separate us. At the end of our historical, biblical, and doctrinal study we do not find any irreducible incompatibilities, despite some real theological and practical divergences.*

We accept unanimously what the creed has passed down to us: it teaches that Jesus "was conceived by the Holy Spirit and born of the Virgin Mary." We have also accepted the testimony of the scriptures. We have regarded Mary as being at the heart of the development of Christ's life in his body the church. This vision is legitimate because it is based on the article of faith that is part of the Apostles' Creed in the words "communion of saints."

336. Where, then, is the continuing difficulty? For Protestants it resides undoubtedly in some of the motifs used in speaking of Mary as Catholics do. But even more it is the appeal to tradition, to the development of dogma, and to the role of the magisterium that causes difficulty, here as elsewhere.

For Catholics the difficulty is doubtless an overly restrictive Protestant reading of the witness of scripture, and also, and perhaps above all, a Protestant resistance to the realm of affectivity, a resistance preserved over the centuries by ceaseless controversies on the Virgin Mary.

Yet our entire work has shown that nothing about Mary allows her to be made the symbol of what separates us.

337. Well, then, is everything now settled? Certainly not! But we accept a common standard: that Mary is never to be separated from her Son and that the "servant of the Lord," for whom "the Mighty One has done great things," glorifies her Son as her Savior and ours. We contemplate Christ in the very mystery of the cross. According to St. John, everything was "finished" after Jesus had entrusted his mother and his disciple to each other. Since we find Mary thus present in God's plan and at the very beginning of the communion of saints, we think that both sides, together with the cloud of witnesses in the history of salvation, are called to an ongoing conversion to Jesus the Christ, who was "conceived by the Holy Spirit and born of the Virgin Mary."

338. At this point we hand over to the attention and prayer of our readers the task of discovering this journey in which they are invited to share. "To the only wise God, through Jesus Christ, to whom be the glory forever" (Rom 17:27).

Appendix I

On the Dogmas of the Immaculate Conception and the Assumption

THE IMMACULATE CONCEPTION

Here, first of all, is the statement of the dogma as defined by Pope Pius IX on December 8, 1854:

> We declare, pronounce and define: the doctrine which holds that the most Blessed Virgin Mary was, from the first moment of her conception, by the singular grace and privilege of almighty God and in view of the merits of Christ Jesus the Saviour of the human race, preserved immune from all stain of original sin, is revealed by God and, therefore, firmly and constantly to be believed by all the faithful. (Bull *Ineffabilis Deus*; DS 2803; ND 709)

This passage calls for some remarks:

–The doctrine of the Immaculate Conception is here the subject of a solemn definition and receives the status of a doctrine "revealed by God." In the pope's own commentary on this definition, he nevertheless emphasizes the continuity of the dogma with the faith of the church as expressed in the liturgical feasts and the teaching of the Fathers and some popes. Moreover, although he refers to several texts of scripture (Gen 3:15; Luke 1:28 and 1:42), he does not argue directly from the Bible; he does acknowledge the doctrine as having been "in the judgment of the Fathers, set down in the divine scriptures."

–The definition proper does not use the term "Immaculate Conception." Nor does it identify the "first moment" of conception; it does, however, maintain that from the "first moment" Mary was preserved from sin.

–Over a century after the definition of Pius IX, the Second Vatican Council stated the mystery of the Immaculate Conception in words that are less "Latin" and bear the impress more of the traditional language of the East:

> It is no wonder...that it was customary for the Fathers to refer to the Mother of God as all holy and free from every stain of sin, as though fashioned by the Holy Spirit and formed as a new creature. Enriched from the first instant of her conception with the splendor of an entirely unique holiness, the virgin of Nazareth is hailed by the heralding angel, by divine command, as "full of grace" (cf. Luke 1:28). (*Lumen Gentium* 56)

THE ASSUMPTION

Here is how Pius XII defined the dogma of the Assumption in the Apostolic Constitution *Munificentissimus Deus* of November 1, 1950:

> By the authority of our Lord Jesus Christ, of the blessed apostles Peter and Paul, and by our own authority, we proclaim, declare and define as a dogma revealed by God: the Immaculate Mother of God, Mary ever Virgin, when the course of her earthly life was finished, was taken up body and soul into the glory of heaven. (DS 3903; ND 715)

Here again, a few comments may be useful:

–The beginning of the definition is an implicit reference to the definition of papal infallibility that was proclaimed in 1870.

–The definition suggests the link between the Assumption and the mysteries of the Immaculate Conception, the divine maternity, and the perpetual virginity.

–The difference between the words "was taken up" (which is a passive verb) and the words used in the Creed for the departure of

Christ ("ascended into heaven") shows that the Assumption of the Virgin is not to be confused with the Ascension of Christ.

—The final words ("was taken up body and soul into the glory of heaven") signal not a change of place but rather a transformation of Mary's body and the passage of her entire being into the "glorious" state in which she is united with the glorious body of her Son.

—In his presentation of the dogma Pius XII does not argue directly from scripture but invokes scripture via the tradition and in light of the bond uniting Mary to her Son.

—Vatican Council II repeats the definition of Pius XII but emphasizes even more the perpetual bond between Mary and her glorious Son:

> The Immaculate Virgin, preserved from all stain of original sin, was taken up body and soul into heavenly glory, when her earthly life was over, and exalted by the Lord as Queen over all things, that she might be more fully conformed to her Son, the Lord of lords (cf. Apoc. 19:16) and conqueror of sin and death. (*Lumen Gentium* 59)

Appendix II

A Little Anthology of Prayers of the Various Western Churches (Except for the Catholic Church) That Include Mary in Their Prayer to God

PRAYERS OF THE ANGLICAN COMMUNION

From the Preface for the Feasts of the Virgin

And now we give you thanks, because in choosing the blessed Virgin Mary to be the mother of your Son you exalted the little ones and the lowly. Your angel greeted her as highly favored; with all generations we call her blessed and with her we rejoice and we magnify your holy name.

Prayer for the Feasts of the Virgin

O God, who have taken to yourself the blessed Virgin Mary, the mother of your Son, grant us to have a part with her in the glory of your eternal kingdom, for we too have been redeemed by the blood of Christ.

PRAYERS OF THE LUTHERAN CHURCHES OF FRANCE

(Liturgy of Sundays and Feasts, February, 1983)

Prayers for the Feasts of the Virgin

Annunciation (March 25 or during Advent)

Lord our God, by the voice of the angel Gabriel you made known to us the incarnation of your Son. Pour out your grace into our hearts so that, following him in his suffering and death, we may also come to the glory of the resurrection through Jesus Christ, your Son, our Lord, who lives and reigns with you, Father, and the Holy Spirit, one God for ever and ever.[1]

Visitation (July 2 or during Advent)

God our Father, through your Spirit you led the Virgin Mary to Elizabeth in order that together they might rejoice in the coming of your Son. Direct our steps as well, in order that we may bring to the world the joy of him who became poor for our sake, Jesus Christ, you Son, our Lord, who lives and reigns with you, Father, and the Holy Spirit, one God for ever and ever.

Preface for the Season of Advent

It is truly right and good, always and everywhere to give you glory and offer you our thanksgiving, most holy Father, eternal and almighty God, through Christ our Lord. He it is of whom all the prophets sang; the Virgin Mary awaited him with love, and John the Baptist proclaimed his coming and revealed his presence. It is he who grants us the joy of already entering into the mystery of Christmas so that when he comes, he may find us waiting in prayer and filled with joy.[2]

For the Fourth Sunday of Advent

Blessed be you through her who is blessed beyond all women; blessed be you because she believed; blessed be you for allowing your servant to open herself to your word and to bear him who created the worlds; blessed be you because through her your Son was able to take our flesh and offer the gift which alone is effective: "Behold, I have come to do your will." (Prayer for the Sunday Liturgy—Lutheran Domestic Mission, 1991)

Anamnesis for the Feast of Christmas

God our Father,
we celebrate the coming of your Son.
Like Mary, we preserve in our hearts
the memory of his birth.
We recall his words and his actions,
his passion and his cross.
His present life is our joy, his return our hope.
In his name we dare to pray: Our Father....

PRAYERS OF THE REFORMED CHURCH

Liturgy of the Reformed Church of France

Father,
you who spoke with Moses face to face,
who made the prophets cry and weep,
who made the psalms well up from your people
and whispered the wisdom of the proverbs to them
You, the living God who placed the *Magnificat*
on the lips of Mary
and the confession of Christ on those of Peter,
You who uttered your Word
as a human word in the life of your Son:
through your Holy Spirit
make these words alive at this hour;

let them become for us your Word.
Amen. (Liturgy of the Reformed Church of France, 1996)

Prayer of the Lord's Supper

We give you thanks, God our Father:

From the beginning, by your Word and the breath of your Spirit, you brought into being the world and its splendor.

You created man in your image and made a covenant with him;

You chose a people for yourself so that through them all the nations of the world might be blessed.

Through your Spirit you caused your Son to be born of the Virgin Mary; he became our brother and lived a life of love of you even to death on the cross.

By the power of your Spirit you raised him from the dead; you made him the head of the Church and Savior of the world....(Experimental "Orange" Liturgy of the Reformed Church of France, 1982)

Hymnals of the Reformed Church of France

No. 171: I magnify God (Magnificat)

1. I magnify God and sing with gladness,
for my Savior stoops to my weakness;
he has seen to it that henceforth
they shall forever call his servant blessed.
2. The Almighty has done marvelous things for me.
Holy is his name! His love is everlasting.
His mighty arm is always at work
for those who do his holy will.
3. He scatters the thoughts of the proud;
he casts down the conceited from their thrones;
he raises up the poor and feeds them;
he sends the rich away with nothing.
4. God keeps his tender love for Israel;
faithful to his promise, he aids it;
for Abraham and his descendants

God is Savior till the end of time.[3] (*Arc en cul* and *Nos coeurs te chantent*, July, 1994)

From a Eucharistic Prayer on the Banquet at Cana

What simplicity, what trust, Lord,
are shown in Mary's words!
–A few words to tell you of a situation that worries her:
"They have no more wine."
–A few words to tell the servants of her confidence:
"Do whatever he tells you."
Yet we are so wordy in our prayers,
so blind to the signs of your presence.

Here we are, invited to your meal,
but what do we know of your life
in this bread and this wine?
What do we know of the grace you have for us?

But let your Spirit come
–and we shall see your presence at the center of this meal
–we shall hear your words sounding in the gospel
–we shall discern your body and your blood
in this bread and this wine....(Pastor Antoine Nouis, La galette et la cruche, Réveil Publications, 1993)

List of Participants

The following contributed to the writing of this work during meetings from 1991 to 1997

Father Jean-Noël Aletti
Pastor François Altermath
Father René Beaupère
Pastor André Benoit
Pastor Alain Blancy
Pastor Daniel Bourguet
Pastor Marc Chambron
Father Bruno Chenu
Father Henri Denis
Father Michel Fédou
Pastor Flemming Fleinert-Jensen
Pastor Michel Freychet
Pastor Daniel Fricker
Father Paul Gay
Father Claude Gerest
Father Étienne Goutagny
Father Pierre Gressot
Pastor Gottfried Hammann
Father Joseph Hoffmann
Father Maurice Jourjon
Pastor Guy Lasserre
Father Pierre Lathuilière
Father Marie Leblanc
Pastor Michel Leplay
Pastor Louis Lévrier
Father Robert Liotard
Father Guy Lourmande
Pastor Alain Martin
Pastor Alain Massini
Pastor Willy-René Nussbaum
Pastor Jacques-Noël Pérès
Father René Remise
Pastor Antoine Reymond
Father Bernard Sesboüé
Father Damien Sicard
Pastor Jean Tartier
Pastor Denis Vatinel
Pastor Jean-Marc Viollet
Father Pierre Vuichard
Pastor Gaston Westphal

Abbreviations Used in the Notes

CO	*Calvini opera quae supersunt omnia*, ed. Baum, Cunitz, and Reuss. Corpus Reformatorum. Braunschweig: Schwetske, 1963–1900.
DC	La Documentation catholique, Paris.
DS	*Enchiridion Symbolorum, definitionum et declarationum de rebus fidei et morum*, ed. H. Denzinger and A. Schönmetzer. 32nd ed. Freiburg: Herder, 1963.
DSp	*Dictionnaire de spiritualité*. Paris: Beauchesne.
LG	*Lumen Gentium*: Constitution of Vatican Council II on the Church.
Mansi	*Sacrorum conciliorum nova et amplissima collectio*. Florence and Venice, 1759–98. Reprint and continuation by J.-B. Martin and L. Petit. 53 vols. Paris: Welter, 1901–27.
ND	*The Christian Faith in the Doctrinal Documents of the Catholic Church*, ed. J. Neuner and J. Dupuis. Revised edition. Staten Island, NY: Alba House, 1982.
PG	*Patrologia graeca*, ed. J.-P. Migne. Paris.
PL	*Patrologia latina*, ed. J.-P. Migne. Paris.
RAM	*Revue d'ascétique et de mystique*. Toulouse.
SC	*Sources chrétiennes*. Lyons-Paris: Cerf.
TRE	*Theologische Realenzyklopädie*. Berlin-New York: de Gruyter.
UR	*Unitatis redintegratio*: Decree of Vatican Council II on Ecumenism.
WA	*Weimarer Ausgabe*: Complete German edition of the works of Luther. Weimar: H. Böhlaus, 1883.

Notes

PART I
PRESENTATION

1. See *Pour la communion des Églises, l'apport du Groupe des Dombes 1937–1987* (Paris: Centurion, 1988), which contains all the earlier documents except for the most recent; the latter constitute a second volume: *Pour la conversion des Églises* (Paris: Centurion, 1991).

INTRODUCTION

1. Paris: Centurion, 1991.

CHAPTER 1

1. Ignatius of Antioch (d. ca. 117), Ephesians 18, 2 (SC 10bis, 87); see *Magnesians* 11; *Trallians* 9, 1; *Smyrnaeans* 1, 1–2.

2. Irenaeus of Lyons, *Demonstration of the Apostolic Preaching* 33 (SC 406, 31).

3. Irenaeus, *Against the Heresies* 1, 10. 2, French trans. A. Rousseau (Paris: Cerf, 1984) 66.

4. The Greek word *ICHTHYS*, "fish," contains the initials (in Greek) of the words "Jesus Christ, Son of God, Savior." The fish thus became a symbolic way of naming Christ, and the play on words is found in ancient inscriptions. Epitaph of Abercius: "Faith was everywhere my guide and everywhere served me as food: a fish from a wellspring, very large and pure, caught by a holy Virgin." Epitaph of Pectorius: "You receive the fish in the

palms of your hands." These inscriptions are translated in: L. Deiss, *Springtime of the Liturgy: Liturgical Texts of the First Four Centuries* (Collegeville: Liturgical Press, 1979) 260–2.

5. See the passage from Ignatius of Antioch, *Ephesians* 18, 2, that was cited in section 10.

6. Irenaeus, *Against the Heresies* 3, 21, 4 (Rousseau, 377).

7. Augustine, *Holy Virginity* 6, 6; trans. by R. Kearney, *Marriage and Virginity* (The Works of Saint Augustine I, 9; Hyde Park, N.Y.: New City Press, 1999) 71.

8. Tertullian in particular.

9. Origen, *Commentaire sur saint Jean* 1, 4 (SC 120, 71).

10. *DS* 427; trans. *ND* 620/6.

11. Especially on the occasion of the fifteenth centenary of Ephesus (1931) and in the form of a feast (October 11) that has now recovered its ancient place on January 1.

12. Augustine, *Holy Virginity* 6, 6 (ET 70).

13. Athanasius, *Letter to Virgins*; see *RAM* 31 (1955) 144–71.

14. Augustine, *Holy Virginity* 5, 5 (ET 70).

15. Augustine, *Nature and Grace* 36, 42; trans. by R. J. Teske, *Answer to the Pelagians* (The Works of Saint Augustine I, 23; Hyde Park, N.Y.: New City Press, 1997) 246.

16. Ibid.

17. See G. Jouassard, "L'interprétation par Cyrille d'Alexandrie de la scène de Marie au pied de la Croix," in the collective work, *Virgo immaculata* (Rome, 1955) 32.

18. Augustine, *Unfinished Work in Answer to Julian* 4, 134; trans. R. J. Teske, *Answer to the Pelagians, III* (The Works of Saint Augustine I, 25; Hyde Park, N.Y.: New City Press, 1999) 500.

19. Andrew of Crete, *Sermon on the Birth of Mary* 1 (PG 97:812A).

20. John Damascene, *Second Homily on the Dormition* 3 (SC 80, 132–33).

21. Papyrus in the John Rylands Library; perhaps predates Ephesus (431).

22. One should "not be sitting" *(akathistos)* while singing the twenty-four stanzas. Here are some of its phrases: "Hail! the whole world's redeeming. Hail! God's goodness unto mankind" (V); "Hail! who drivest from his realm the foe of men....Hail! who redeemest from pagan rites" (IX); "Hail! rock that waterest the thirsting for life....Hail! food superceding the manna" (XI). Text and translation by G. G. Meersseman, O.P., *The Acathistos Hymn:*

Hymn of Praise to the Mother of God (Fribourg, Switzerland.: University Press, 1958) 39, 47, and 51.

23. Ambrose of Milan, *Sur l'évangile de Luc* 10, 132 (*SC* 52, 200); also *Letter* 63, 110 (*PL* 16:1218C).

24. Irenaeus, *Against the Heresies* 3, 22, 4 (Rousseau, 385–86).

25. Ibid., 5, 19, 1 (Rousseau, 626).

26. John Chrysostom, a "literalist," says: "This law holds everywhere in the scriptures: whenever it uses allegory, it also interprets the allegory, in order to keep the unbridled desire of lovers of allegorical interpretation from going naively astray and finding it everywhere" (*Commentary on Isaiah* 5, 3).

27. In Rome, ca. 700: Annunciation, Dormition, Nativity, Purification. The East celebrated the four feasts attested for Rome, but added December 9, the feast of Anne's conception of Mary. Light has been shed on the origins of the feast of the *Dormition by Simon Claude Mimouni's stimulating study: Dormition et Assomption de Marie, histoire des traditions anciennes* (Paris: Beauchesne, 1995).

28. We must avoid *defining* Christian apocryphal literature *in relation to* the New Testament canon, as if it formed a competing or even simply complementary body of works. The tendency today is to view this literature rather as the written form of a particular stage of historical traditions or of a set of legends that did not have the authority of the canon of scripture.

29. See *Protevangelium of James* 8, 1, in W. Schneemelcher (ed.), *New Testament Apocrypha* I (Louisville: Westminster/John Knox Press, 1991) 429; *The Questions of Bartholomew* II, 15 (ibid., 544).

30. See *Protevangelium of James* 20, 1 (Schneemelcher I, 434); *Gospel of Pseudo-Matthew* 13, 4.

31. See Gregory Palamas, *Homily 18 on the Women Bringing Myrrh* 5.

32. See the *History of Joseph the Carpenter* 20, 8.

33. See Mimouni, *Dormition et Assomption* (note 27, above).

34. By "dormition" these texts understand the death of Mary, with the apostles around her, while an angel—or even the risen Christ, who then entrusts her to Michael—receives her soul and raises it to glory, her body being placed in a tomb. The "assumption," which does not, of itself, imply Mary's death, but may in fact follow upon it, signifies her elevation, body and soul, into glory, while saying nothing about her burial.

35. H. Grote, "Maria/Marienfrömmigkeit," *TRE* 22, 123–24.

36. We shall return to this subject in chapter II, nos. 276–88.

37. This statement has been attributed to Bernard of Clairvaux, but without reference to any explicit passage. Bernard's Marian theology is, paradoxically, focused on the humility of the mother of Christ more than on her

exaltation. In any case, the statement does well describe the invasive Marian piety of that time.

38. Grote (note 35) 126–28.

39. *Mansi* 29, 182f.; *DTC* 7/1. 1113.

40. Sixtus IV, *On the Immaculate Conception;* text in *DS* 1400.

41. See, further on, section 152, note 9.

42. See his *Sermon for the Day of the Lord's Annunciation* (*PL* 185/1:115ff.); *Panegyric on the Blessed Virgin, Mother of God* (*PL* 184:1009ff. and 1020). In these sermons, Bernard extols the Virgin Mary as Virgin of virgins, Wisdom, Mother of beautiful love, Mother of mercy, my Lady (*mi Domina* or *Domina mea*), Spouse, Mother of God, Mediatrix, sweet Perfume, White Rose for virginity, Red Rose for charity. But she possesses these titles only in function of her Son. According to Bernard, we have but one mother on earth as we have but one Father in heaven. See R. Winling, the Carmelites of Mazille, and A.-G. Hamman, *Le cantique des cantiques d'Origène à saint Bernard* (Paris: Desclée de Brouwer, 1983) 183–88.

43. See Grote (note 35) 130–31.

44. This period saw the beginning of such movements as *Église et liturgie* in French-speaking Switzerland and the St. Michael Confraternity in Germany. This Lutheran or Reformed renewal in liturgy and Mariology was intended as a step toward ecumenical dialogue.

45. Walter Tappolet, *Das Marienlob der Reformatoren* (Tübingen, 1962); Max Thurian, *Mary, Mother of All Christians,* trans. N. Cryer (New York, 1963).

46. "Let pastors not engage in quarreling over these feasts. Let each be free to celebrate those which his parishioners want. Let them honor, above all else, the Sundays, the feasts of the Annunciation, the Purification, and the Visitation, the feasts of St. John the Baptist, St. Michael, the apostles, and St. Mary Magdalene" (WA 26, 222.25—233.1). On the Marian feasts mentioned Luther preached about 80 sermons on Mary.

47. See, among other passages, WA 27, 242.4 (1528); 27, 475.25-26 (1528); 29, 169.8 (1539).

48. "We too are made pregnant by the Holy Spirit and receive Christ into ourselves spiritually through faith" (WA 9, 625.22).

49. WA 32, 296.16–19.

50. "Die Gottesmutter," WA 7, 572.33—573.1; see Tappolet (note 45, above) 110ff.

51. See WA 7, 575.8–12.

52. See WA 49, 492–98.

53. "So great is the comfort and overflowing kindness of God that human beings can, if they believe, take advantage of this great treasure: that Mary is their true mother, Christ their brother, and God their father" (*WA* 10/I, 72.19–73.2).

54. *WA* 1, 107.22-25.

55. *WA* 4, 234.5-8.

56. See M. Lienhard, *Au coeur de la foi de Luther: Jésus Christ* (Paris: Desclée, 1991) 59.

57. *WA* 10/III, 331.4-11.

58. *WA* 10/III, 268,13-18.

59. See *WA* 52, 681.6-31 (1544).

60. See *WA* 10/I/1, 62.1763.10.

61. According to Luther, the Marian devotion of his times was unfortunately a product of a distortion of Christology: Christ, seen as "judge and executioner" (*WA* 10/III, 357.231), gave rise to a Mary who was "exclusively sweetness and love."

62. *Defense*, art. XXI: "On the Invocation of the Saints," in A. Birmelé and M. Lienhard, *La foi des Églises luthériennes* (Paris: Cerf; Geneva: Labor et Fides, 1991) no. 278.

63. Ibid., no. 369.

64. Ibid., no. 278.

65. Ibid., no. 390.

66. "The miracle is that she was a virgin before and after the birth [of Christ]" (Zwinglis Werke 6/1, 288.10–289.5). As in Luther, so Zwingli's Christocentrism implies a veneration of Mary that flows from adoration of Christ and honors Christ (ZW 5, 188.10-14). See Tappolet (note 45, above) 251.

67. ZW 1, 412.1-8.

68. Let Mary not turn believers away from the wretched social conditions experienced "by young girls and women whose beauty or poverty place them in danger" (ZW 3, 52.14).

69. Calvin applies the words "and Mary kept all these things in her heart" (Luke 2:51) to Joseph as well (CO 46, col. 481).

70. See *Institutes of the Christian Religion*, trans. F. L. Battles (Library of Christian Classics 20-21; Philadelphia: Westminster, 1960) IV, 1, 4 (ET 1016); she is "mother of all those into whose bosom God is pleased to gather his sons" (IV, 1, 1; ET 1012); she "keeps us under her care and guidance" (IV, 1, 4; ET 1016); we are "nourished by her help and ministry" (IV, 1, 1; ET 1012).

71. CO 46, col. 111.

72. Even the apostles are her students; see CO 46, col. 63. According to Calvin, this formative role of Mary was shown at the wedding feast of Cana: "Do whatever he tells you!" As a good teacher, she refers people to Christ and his word; we ought to do the same: "Thus, following the example of the Virgin, let us learn in the same way to hear what is taught us in the word of God and to read this word with such zeal that we give it a dwelling place in our hearts and let it take root there" (CO 46, col. 482).

73. Cajetan. *Thirty-nine Articles on the Praise and Veneration of the Virgin Mary* (1525); see *Handbuch der Marienkunde*, ed. W. Beinert and H. Petri (Regensburg: Pustet, 1984) 206.

74. See Michel de Saint-Augustin (d. 1684) and his *Vita mariaeformis et mariana in Maria propter Mariam*, published in 1669; according to this work, "Mary is the means and the strongest bond of the soul with God" (ch. 12).

75. See *DSp* 10 (Paris: Beauchesne, 1980) cols. 461–62.

76. Henri-Marie Boudon (1624–1702), *Dieu seul, ou le saint esclavage de l'admirable Mère de Dieu* (Paris, 1667), in his *Oeuvres complètes*, ed. Migne, 2 (1857) col. 378.

77. See *DSp* 10, cols. 460ff.

78. See ibid., cols. 462, 464.

79. See, e.g., the *Neuvième lettre écrite à un provincial par un de ses amis* (July 1656), in Pascal, *Oeuvres complètes* (Paris: Pléiade, NRF, Gallimard, 1954) 753ff.

80. In his sermon on the *Conception de la Sainte Vierge* (December 8, 1669); see *DSp* 10, col. 463.

81. Antoine Godeau, in his *L'assomption de la Vierge*; see *DTC* 6 (1920) cols. 1470–71.

82. See de Montfort's *Traité de la vraie dévotion à la Sainte Vierge* (written before 1716 but published only in the nineteenth century), in his *Oeuvres complètes* (Paris, 1966).

83. French-speaking members of the Reformed Churches (like the Lutherans) claimed the name "Catholic" (but with ever less insistence) down to the beginning of the nineteenth century. A typical example can be seen in the *Later Helvetic Confession* (1556), which is described on its title page as "Confession and Plain Exposition of the true faith and *catholic* articles" of the churches in Switzerland, and in the title of chapter 18: "On the Holy and *Catholic* Church of God." From the historical standpoint, "catholicity" is to the one church what "Reformed" (or "Lutheran") is to the confessional church; the same has been true of the "Roman Catholic" Church beginning in the sixteenth century.

84. See Émile G. Léonard, *Histoire générale du protestantisme* II (Paris: Presses universitaires de France, 1961) 320.

85. In 1639, French theologian André Rivet (d. 1651), the dean of the theology faculty in Leiden (Netherlands) and acknowledged guardian of Reformed orthodoxy, wrote a Latin work on the Virgin Mary in which he developed the same themes as Drelincourt: Rivet's work was titled *Apologia pro sanctissima virgine Maria matre Domini, adv. veteres et novos antidicomarianitas, Collyridianos et Christiano-categoros, Lib. II absoluta.*

86. *De ingeniorum moderatione in religionis negotio* (Paris, 1714); see *DTC* 10/2, col. 1551, and *DSp* 10, col. 467.

87. On the situation see R. Laurentin, *La question mariale* (Paris: Seuil, 1963).

88. *Signum magnum*, 1967 (*DC*, no. 1495 [1967] 961–72) and *Marialis cultus*, 1974 (*DC* no. 1651 [1974] 301–9).

89. See, e.g., J. Bosc, P. Bourget, P. Maury, and H. Roux, *Le protestantisme et la Vierge Marie* (Paris: "Je sers," 1950); P. Petit, *Lourdes, les protestants, la tradition chrétienne* (Paris: Les Bergers et les mages, 1958).

90. We are here simply reporting the historical situation; an analysis of the disagreement on these points will be given in Chapter 3, sections 207–27.

91. See A. and F. Dumas, *Marie de Nazareth* (Geneva: Labor et Fides, 1989).

92. The document mixes up the immaculate conception with the virginal conception of Jesus. See below, section 300, note 10.

93. A. Wohlfahrt, *Le cep et les sarments. Catéchisme à l'usage de l'Église de la Confession d'Augsbourg* (Strasbourg: Éd. Oberlin, 1965).

94. *Liturgie des dimanches et fêtes de l'ANELF* (1983) 195, 197, 219; *Liturgie expérimentale de l'ERF* (the "Orange" liturgy), Prayer for the Lord's Supper, p. 44.

CHAPTER 2

1. By "creed" we mean here the Apostles' Creed and the Nicene-Constantinopolitan Creed.

2. In Freud's view, some desire is always at the root of both "sublimation" and "idealization." In "sublimation," however, the desire accepts the loss of its immediate object and is shifted to a different object; it projects on the latter the elements of pleasure or goodness that had been attributed to the original object. In "idealization," on the other hand, the desire is not

symbolically detached from its immediate object; the person rejects this loss and, aided by its drive to keep control, fabricates an object in keeping with its representation of the original object. See S. Nobécourt-Granier, "Ni saintes ni sorcières, les femme deviennent dans la foi en Dieu," *Incroyance et Foi,* no., 39 (fall, 1986) 19–29; idem, "Freud et la virginité," in the collective work *La première fois* (Paris: Ramsay, 1981) 401–43; Dominique Stein, "Figures de Marie et voeux de l'inconscient," *Femmes et hommes dans l'Église* (Bulletin international), no. 7 (December, 1981).

3. See F. Quéré, *Marie* (Paris: Desclée De Brouwer, 1996) 55–58.

4. Recall here that in the Old Testament the Books of Kings very often mention the mothers of the kings of the Davidic dynasty (see 1 Kgs 2:19; 11:26; 14:21; and so on).

5. F. Quéré, *Jésus enfant* (Paris: Desclée, 1992) 130.

6. We shall cite here Acts 1:14, the only passage of this book that mentions Mary, although the scene concerns rather the church and belongs under the third article of the creed.

7. Matthew cites Isa 7:14 according to the Septuagint, which translates the Hebrew *almah* as "virgin."

8. The extratestamental literature contains a work that makes it possible to establish a connection between Jewish traditions and the virginal birth of Jesus. The *(Slavonic Apocalypse of) Enoch* reports that Spanim, mother of Melchizedek, conceived her child without the intervention of a man (*2 Enoch* 71); text in J. H. Charlesworth (ed.), *The Old Testament Pseudepigrapha* 2 (New York: Doubleday, 1983) 204.

9. Mary is *kecharitômenê,* "filled with grace," not "full of grace," this being the prerogative of the Word made flesh, who is "full of grace and truth" (*plêrês charitos kai alêtheias,* John 1:14).

10. The doctrinal dispute about the brothers and sisters of Jesus will be studied in Chapter 3, nos. 228–233.

11. The verb "keep" *(têreô)* in Luke 2:51 is the same verb as in 2:19, but the prefix is different (*diatêreô* instead of *syntêreô*).

12. Without excluding other forms of worship, we use the word "liturgy" here to refer primarily to the rite of the Mass or worship (word and sacrament); this is almost identical in the various rites and confessions.

13. See the great heavenly liturgy in Rev 4–5.

14. See the Roman Canon of the Roman liturgy.

15. The image of a race that is evoked in Heb 12:1–2 speaks of support from those who have already died: they surround us, thus showing their concern and support in the struggles which others must still endure. These

witnesses do not in any sense compete with the unique role of Christ who is both the starting point and the goal of the race to be run.

16. The prayer *Communicantes* goes back to the sixth century. Ambrose of Milan is witness to a text of which the *Communicantes* is not yet a part (*De sacramentis* 4.21–29; *SC* 25bis [Paris, 1961] 114–16). But in his catecheses Ambrose does mention the Virgin Mary in the context of the Eucharist when he compares the offering of bread and wine by Melchizedek "who had neither father nor mother" with the offering of Jesus (4.12; p. 109).

PART II
CHAPTER 3

1. For the meaning of this term see no. 242 and note 38.

2. In 1992, the commission for Lutheran-Catholic dialogue in the United States published a document titled: *The One Mediator, the Saints, and Mary. Lutherans and Catholics in Dialogue* VIII, ed. H. George Anderson, J. Francis Stafford, and Joseph A. Burgess (Minneapolis: Augsburg), which says: "The goal of ecumenical dialogue is not to eliminate all differences, but to make certain that the remaining differences are consonant with a fundamental consensus in the apostolic faith and therefore legitimate or at least tolerable. Reconciliation is a process admitting of many degrees, leading up to full fellowship in faith, in sacramental worship, and in a structured ecclesial life. It is therefore important to ascertain what bearing the differences have...on the kinds of fellowship just mentioned" (no. 90). We shall several times refer to this work, which is independent of ours but convergent with it. [The text can also be found in *Growing Consensus. Church Dialogues in the United States, 1962–1991*, ed. J. A. Burgess and J. Gros (New York: Paulist Press, 1995) 374–451.]

3. K. Barth, *Kirchliche Dogmatik* I, 2, § 15 (Zurich: EBZ, 1939, p. 154). The German text thus preceded the definition of the Assumption.

4. Ibid., IV, 3, 2, § 71 (Zurich: EBZ, 1939, p. 691).

5. John Paul II, Encyclical *Redemptoris Mater* (March 25, 1987), no. 13.

6. K. Barth, *Kirchliche Dogmatik* I, 2, § 15 (Zurich: EBZ, 1939, p. 160).

7. Jean Bosc, "La Constitution *Lumen Gentium*," in *Vatican II, Points de vue protestants* (Paris: Cerf, 1967), no. 64, p. 44.

8. Jean Bosc, *Le dialogue catholique-protestant* (Paris: La Palatine, 1960) 49.

9. A recent commission, formed at the request of the Holy See in order to answer various requests for the definition of new Marian titles, had this to say: "We must not abandon the theological course taken by Vatican II,

which was unwilling to define any of these titles....The term 'Co-Redemptrix' has not been used in important documents of the teaching of the supreme pontiffs, and this since the time of Pius XII. There are testimonies to the fact this pontiff deliberately avoided using the word....Finally, theologians, especially non-Catholic theologians, have shown themselves sensitive to the ecumenical difficulties a definition of such titles would entail."

The Pontifical Marian Academy had this to say about the response: "The Commission's response, which was deliberately brief, was unanimous and to the point: it is not appropriate to abandon the path taken by Vatican Council II and to move toward the definition of a new dogma." The Academy even voiced its surprise at the request for a dogmatic definition "of a title toward which the magisterium has reservations and which it systematically avoids" (*DC* no. 2164 [1997] 693, 694, and 696).

10. *The One Mediator, the Saints, and Mary*, no. 56.

11. Ibid., no 70: "Both [our Churches] agree on the unique mediatorship of Christ (solus Christus) and the justification for sinners (sola gratia) that Christ provides; they use this doctrine 'as a criterion of authenticity' for the Church's practice with regard to the saints and Mary. The problem, however, is how to affirm the unique mediatorship of Christ so that all the 'mediations' in his Church not only do not detract from, but communicate and extol, his sole mediatorship."

12. See no. 209.

13. See Eph 5:25–27. Paul's text speaks of the church; Luther applies it to believers and to Mary, in his *The Freedom of a Christian, Martin Luther: Selection from His Writings*, ed. J. Dillenberger (New York, 1962) 60.

14. Ibid., 75–77.

15. Augustine, *Letter* 195, 5, 19 (*PL* 33, 880). The passage has become part of the first preface of the saints in the Catholic liturgy. See also his *Confessions* 9, 13, 14 (BA 14, 134); *Homilies on the Gospel of John* 3, 10 (BA 71, 229).

16. See *The One Mediator, the Saints, and Mary*, no. 60: "In Catholic teaching it [the cooperation of Mary and others] implies that from eternity the Father chooses to save for Christ's sake and in a way that involves the free agency of human beings.... These...examples of such involvement or cooperation...are effective because: (a) the Father grants salvation in the Holy Spirit thanks solely to Jesus Christ; (b) the efficacy of this one Mediator is so great as to enable disciples to share freely and actively in his saving work."

17. Ambrose of Milan, *Sur l'Évangile de Luc* 10, 132 (SC 52, 200). See also above, chapter I, no. 26.

18. Vatican II, *Lumen Gentium*, no. 58.

19. See Luther, *The Freedom of a Christian*: "When this [true worship of God] is done, the soul consents to his will. Then it hallows his name and allows itself to be treated according to God's good pleasure for, clinging to God's promises, it does not doubt that he who is true, just, and wise will do, dispose, and provide all things well.

"Is not such a soul most obedient to God on all things by his faith? What commandment is there that such obedience has not completely fulfilled? What more complete fulfillment is there than obedience in all things? This obedience, however, is not rendered by works, but by faith alone" (Dillenberger, 59).

20. Alexandre Vinet, *Homilétique, ou Théorie de la prédication* (Paris, 1853) 27–8.

21. Augustine, Sermon 169, 11, 13.

22. *The One Mediator, the Saints, and Mary* no. 61: "The cooperative roles that Jesus Christ gives to his disciples on earth through the centuries are the fruit of his mediation and contribute to others' reception of grace he mediates."

23. See Luther, *The Freedom of a Christian*: "Why should I not therefore freely, joyfully, with all my heart and with an eager will do all things which I know are pleasing and acceptable to such a Father who has overwhelmed me with his inestimable riches? I will therefor give myself *as a Christ to my neighbor*, just as Christ offered himself to me....

"Hence, as our heavenly Father has in Christ freely come to our aid, we also ought freely to help our neighbor through our body and its works, and each one should *become as it were a Christ to the other....*

"We are altogether ignorant of our own name and do not know why we are Christians or bear the name of Christians. Surely we are named after Christ, not because he is absent from us, but because he dwells in us, that is, because we believe in him and *are Christs one to another* and do to our neighbor as Christ does to us" (Dillenberger, 75–76; italics added).

24. See what Alexandre Vinet wrote about the church: "It does nothing by itself, but it does through him everything that he did on earth. It continues his work, but through him and for him. It is the entire body, it is not the head" (in *Le fidèle achevant la souffrance du Christ. Fragment d'un discours de* M. *Vinet* [Lausanne, 1848] 5).

25. See the conclusions offered on this point in nos. 295 and 323–24.

26. See, e.g., the statement of the Joint Catholic-Protestant Commission in France: "The Church is able to give only because it has first received. It can be a reconciler only because it has first been reconciled. It is always first of all a passive recipient of the grace of God. Everything it does refers back to

this source which does not belong to it and in relation to which it must be transparent....The difference between us, therefore, has to do not with the fact that the Church is an instrument in the transmission of salvation, but with the *nature of this instrumentality: Is the Church sanctified in such a way that it becomes itself a sanctifying subject?*" (Comité mixte catholique-protestant en France, Consensus oecuménique et différence fondamentale [Paris: Centurion, 1987], no. 11, pp. 19–20).

27. See nos. 185–89.

28. See F. Refoulé, *Les frères et soeurs de Jesus: frères ou cousins?* (Paris: Desclée De Brouwer, 1995); P. Grelot, *Jésus de Nazareth, Christ et Seigneur* I (Paris-Montreal: Cerf/Novalis, 1997) 294–301; idem, "Les noms de parenté dans le livre de Tobie," Revue de Qumran 17 (1996) 327–37; F. Quéré, *Les femmes de l'Évangile* (Paris: Seuil, 1982); E. Cuvillier, *Qui donc es-tu, Marie? Les différents visages de la mère de Jésus dans le Nouveau Testament* (Paris: Éditions du Moulin, 1994).

29. The Greek word *adelphos* can mean a close relation or cousin; thus in the LXX Lot is called the "brother" of Abraham (Gen 13:8), and Laban and Jacob are said to be "brothers" (Gen 29:15). Nor should we forget the Old Testament use of the word "brother" for a member of the people of God (Exod 2:11; etc.). Philo also attests to this broader meaning. The New Testament use of the word for members of a community is comparable to its modern use in the word "brotherhood." According to Kittel,"in some non-Christian circles the word 'brother' could refer to members of a community who had no ties of blood; e.g., in Memphis, according to a Greek inscription (*Inscriptiones Graecae*, 1873ff., XIV 956 B, llf alpha)."

30. See no. 19.

31. More specifically, see Calvin who urges (CO 45 [1891] col. 70) that this point not be made "a matter of curiosity contrary to the scriptures," and who observes in 1553, in connection with John 2:12: "In any case, it is very well known that in Hebrew the word 'brothers' is applied to all the cousins and relatives" (*Commentaires sur le Nouveau Testament* II. *Évangile selon saint Jean* [Geneva: Labor et Fides, 1968] 61–62). For Luther's position see no. 55.

32. See A. Schlatter, *Marien-Reden* (Velbert i. Rheinland: Freizeiten Verlag, 1927); H. Asmussen, *Maria die Mutter Gottes* (Stuttgart: Evangelisches Verlagswerk, 1950) 28ff.; W. Stählin, "Maria die Mutter des Herrn, Ihr biblisches Bild," in his *Symbolon. Gesammelte Aufsätze* I, 222–35; M. Thurian, frère de Taizé, *Mary, Mother of All Christians*, trans. N. B. Cryer (New York, 1963); L. Vischer, *Ökumenische Skizzen* (Franfurt a. M.: Lembeck, 1972) 109–23;

H. Ott, "Steht Maria zwischen den Konfessionen?" in *In necessariis unitas* (Paris: Cerf, 1984) 305–19.

33. See the conclusions offered on this subject in nos. 301–302 and 327.

34. In Appendix I of the present document the reader will find the texts of the dogmatic definitions of the Immaculate Conception and the Assumption, along with some explanatory observations.

35. See P. N. Trembelas, *Dogmatique de l'Église orthodoxe catholique* II (Chevetogne: Éditions de Chevetogne, and Paris: Desclée De Brouwer, 1967) 229–33; A. Kniazeff, *La Mère de Dieu dans l'Église orthodoxe* (Paris: Cerf, 1990) 124ff.

36. On the distinction between the two words see no. 37 and note 33.

37. See J. Meyendorff, *Initiation à la théologie byzantine* (Paris: Cerf, 1975) 192ff. (original sin) and 198ff. (the new Eve).

38. "In ecumenical dialogue, Catholic theologians....should remember that in Catholic doctrine there exists an order or 'hierarchy' of truths, since they vary in their relation to the foundation of the Christian faith" (*UR* 11). When Msgr. Pangrazio explained the idea of a "hierarchy" of truths at Vatican II, he distinguished between truths that belong to the *order of ends* (such as the Trinity) and those that belong to the *order of means* (such as the hierarchic structure of the church). The conciliar text, however, stresses rather the relation of each truth to the "foundation" of the faith, that is, the revelation of God as Savior in Jesus Christ through the gift of the Spirit. The place of doctrines in the "hierarchy" of truths must therefore be decided primarily by their (more or less direct) relation to the scriptures and to the statements set down in the creeds.

In an analogous manner, Protestants will distinguish between the major points of faith that belong to the *status confessionis* and other teachings; in the Lutheran tradition in particular, justification by faith is often said to be a criterion that determines whether a doctrine is well founded. Luther and Melanchthon thought that there is a hierarchy in which articles of faith dealing with soteriology (salvation, the Gospel) have a higher place than those dealing with ecclesiology and ethics (works, the Law). The later *Helvetic Confession* of the Reformers distinguishes between things that are indifferent and truths derived from the confession of faith: "[This is] why when indifferent things are added to the confession of faith, they are no longer left to our freedom" (*Confessions et catéchismes de la foi reformée,* ch. 27, p. 300).

39. We think it useful to repeat here, in a dogmatic perspective, some points already made in the historical section (nos. 87–119).

40. Cyril of Alexandria passed a stern judgment on Mary's lack of faith and her "fall" at the foot of the cross: "The poor mother would certainly have thought: 'I gave birth to this man whom they are mocking on the wood. He said that he was himself the true Son of God, the Master of the universe, but he doubtless deceived himself. We must think he deceived himself when he said: "I am the life." How could he be crucified here?'....In speaking of a sword, Simeon was expressing the keenness and strength of the suffering that would lead Mary to such inopportune thoughts, thus setting her weak female mind on the wrong path....I add that even his mother stumbled and fell. She found herself lacking direction, her ideas in confusion....Knowing her thoughts, he [Jesus] entrusted her to that best of mystagogues, his disciple" (*Commentary on John* 12 [*PG* 74, 661b], cited in M. Jouassard, "L'interprétation par Cyrille d'Alexandrie de la scène de Marie au pied de la croix," in Virgo Immaculata [Rome: Academia Mariana Internationalis, 1955] 28–47; citations from 31, 32, and 35).

41. *Unfinished Work in Answer to Julian* 4, 122 (*PL* 45, 1418).

42. See, earlier, nos. 44–45.

43. *DS* 1425–26. Recall that in 1439 the Council of Basel had defined the Immaculate Conception and established the feast on December 8; see no. 45, above.

44. Council of Trent, Session 5, ch. 6 (*DS* 1516; *ND* 513); see no. 70, above.

45. *DS* 2015–17.

46. But belonging in fact to Paschase Radbert, *PL* 30:122–42.

47. *PL* 40:1141–48.

48. See no. 97, above.

49. Of 1181 replies, 1169 were positive and 22 negative. Of the 22, 16 challenged only the timeliness of the definition.

50. In fact, even though the dogma does not take a position on this point, is it possible for us today to imagine that Mary did not experience death, which every other human being experiences and which even the Son of God accepted? See the address of John Paul II to a general audience on June 25, 1997: "Some theologians have maintained that the Virgin was exempted from death and that she passed directly from earthly life to heavenly glory. But this opinion was unknown until the seventeenth century, whereas there exists a common tradition that sees Mary being brought into heavenly glory by way of death" (*DC* 2164 [1997] 656–57).

51. G. Greshake, *Plus fort que la mort* (Paris: Mame, 1979) 92.

52. The Catholic dogma of the Assumption also implies that the Mother of Jesus did not undergo the corruption of the grave: having been

preserved from sin, Mary was also preserved from the corruption that accompanies death (death being understood as a consequence of sin).

53. It is to be noted that the Orthodox speak of this "redemption" as a "purification" rather than a "preservation" from sin.

54. See the opening prayer of the Catholic Mass of the Immaculate Conception: "Father, you prepared the Virgin Mary to be the worthy mother of your Son. You let her share beforehand in the salvation Christ would bring by his death, and kept her sinless from the first moment of her conception."

55. The passive participle "filled with grace" *(kekharitômene)* in Luke 1:28 occurs only here in the New Testament, and we can see in it a sign of a unique gift to Mary. It is, however, the same verb that is used in Eph 1:6 of Christians to whom God had granted his grace *(echaritôsen)*. In our time it would be desirable to avoid the expression "Marian privilege" when speaking of the Immaculate Conception (and the Assumption), in order not to lose sight of the significance of these dogmas for our humanity as such.

56. See the conclusions offered on this point in nos. 296–300 and 326.

57. Luther, *Sermon on the Ave Maria* (1523; *WA* 11, 61).

58. Calvin on Luke 2:15–19 in his twenty-fifth sermon on the *Harmony of the Gospels*, cited in *La Revue réformée* no. 32 (1957, no. 4) 37: "The papists will call the Virgin Mary the 'treasurer of grace'; but they blaspheme God...in wanting her to have the office proper to our Lord Jesus."

59. To give but one example that is extreme by reason of the speaker's unawareness of what he was saying: In a book *L'Immaculée Conception* (Brussels, 1857), Msgr. J. Malou calls Mary "a divine person" or "the fourth person of the Holy Trinity," and this supposedly "according to the Fathers": see R. Laurentin, *Court Traité sur la Vierge Marie* (5th ed.; Paris: Lethielleux, 1967) 87. See, for opposition to the trend, this statement of Newman in his *Apologia pro vita sua*, Ch. 4: "Such devotional manifestations in honor of our Lady had been my great *crux* as regards Catholicism; I say frankly, I do not fully enter into them now; I trust that I do not love her less, because I cannot enter into them. They may be fully explained and defended; but sentiment and taste do not run with logic; they are suitable for Italy, but they are not suitable for England" (ed. C. F. Harrold [New York, 1947] 176).

60. See the conclusions proposed on this point in nos. 307–14 and 328–33.

CHAPTER 4

1. *Mary in the Churches*, ed. H. Küng and J. Moltmann (*Concilium* 168; New York, 1983) xii.

2. *Encyclopédie du protestantisme* (Paris: Cerf and Geneva: Labor et Fides, 1995) 950.

3. See, e.g., the Malta Ecumenical Declaration (1983), in *Unité des chrétiens*, no. 69 (January 1988) 18.

4. See the document several times cited: *The One Mediator, and the Saints, and Mary. Lutherans and Catholics in Dialogue* VIII.

5. That is, it is not possible to maintain a "personal (hypostatic) communication" of the Holy Spirit to the Virgin Mary as L. Boff does in his *Trinité et société* (Paris: Cerf, 1990) 247.

6. Cardinal J. Ratzinger has several times applied this very principle to the dialogue with the East on the Roman primacy: "Rome must not ask of the East, when it comes to the doctrine of the primacy, more than what was formulated and practiced during the first millennium" (*Les principes de la théologie catholique* [Paris: Téqui, 1985] 222). He goes on to say that an agreement could therefore be reached on the basis of a mutual acceptance of the Churches' respective positions as "legitimate and orthodox."

7. Is this not true, for example, of the following passage in the encyclical *Mortalium animos* of 1928? "In matters of faith it is not permitted to make a distinction between *fundamental* and so-called *non-fundamental* articles of faith, as if the first ought to be held by all and the second the faithful are free to accept or not....Therefore, as many as are of Christ give, for example, to the dogma of the Immaculate Conception the same faith they give to the mystery of the Trinity" (trans. R. A. McGowan in *Sixteen Encyclicals of His Holiness Pius XI (1926–37)* (Washington, D.C.: National Catholic Welfare Conference, n.d.) 13 (italics added).

8. See the statement of Pius IX that was included in the definition of 1854: "If, therefore, any persons shall dare to think—which God forbid—otherwise than has been defined by us, let them clearly know that they stand condemned by their own judgment, that they have made shipwreck of their faith and fallen from the unity of the Church" (*DS* 2804; *ND* 2804). This text cannot by any accounting be addressed to Orthodox and Protestant Christians.

9. See Groupe de Dombes, *Pour la conversion des Églies* (Paris: Centurion, 1991), no. 59 and note 1 (p. 41).

10. Popular piety often confuses the virginal conception of Jesus and the Immaculate Conception of Mary herself.

11. See nos. 60–67.

12. Paul VI, Apostolic Exhortation *Marialis Cultus* on Devotion to the Blessed Virgin Mary (February 2, 1974). In the following sections of our text this document will be referred to by its numbered paragraphs.

13. Here is the text:

> The angel of the Lord declared unto Mary
> *and she conceived by the Holy Spirit.
> Hail, Mary....
> "Behold the handmaid of the Lord,
> *let it be done to me according to your word.
> Hail, Mary....
> And the Word was made flesh,
> *and dwelt among us.
> Hail, Mary....
> Pray for us, O holy Mother of God,
> *that we made be made worthy
> of the promises of Christ.
>
> Let us pray. Pour forth, we beseech you, O Lord, your grace into our hearts, that we to whom the incarnation of Christ, your Son, was made known by the message of an angel, may by his passion and cross be brought to the glory of his resurrection, through the same Christ our Lord. Amen!

14. The rosary is made up of five decades, each containing an Our Father, ten Hail Marys, and a trinitarian doxology. The recitation of each decade is accompanied by meditation on one of the mysteries of Christ, which are grouped into three series: the joyful mysteries (Annunciation, Visitation, Nativity, Presentation in the temple, Finding of the Child Jesus in the Temple); the sorrowful mysteries (Agony in the Garden, Scourging, Crowning with Thorns, Carrying of the Cross, Death on the Cross); glorious mysteries (Resurrection, Ascension, Pentecost, Assumption, Crowning of Mary).

15. See Vatican II, *Dei Verbum* 4.

16. John of the Cross, *Ascent of Mount Carmel* II, 20: "Having given us his Son, who is his Word, he has no other word to give to us. He has said everything, once and for all, in this Word alone; he has nothing more, then, to say to us....What he said partially to the prophets he has said entirely in his Son by giving us the Son in his entirety. This is why anyone now wishing to question him or desiring a vision or a revelation would not only be foolish but would insult God by not fastening his gaze solely on Christ, without seek-

ing anything else or any novelty" (trans. from the French text) (passage cited in the *Liturgy of the Hours*, vol. I, p. 212).

17. Benedict XIV, *De servorum Dei beatificatione* II, 32, 11.

18. B. Bobrinskoy, in the collective work *Vraies et fausses apparitions dans l'Église* (Paris: Lethielleux-Bellarmin, 1976) 109.

19. Did not St. Thérèse of the Child Jesus already protest that "we ought not say things" about Mary "which are improbable or which we do not know....If a sermon of the holy Virgin is to please me and do me good, it must make me see her real life, not her supposed life; and I am sure that her real life must have been very simple. Preachers show her as unapproachable; they ought to show her as imitable, bring out her virtues, say that she lived by faith as we do, and give proofs of this from the gospel, where we read: 'They did not understand what he was saying to them'....We know indeed that the holy Virgin is Queen of heaven and earth, but she is more a mother than a queen, and we ought not to say that because of her prerogatives she eclipses the glory of all the saints, just as the rising sun makes the stars disappear. Dear Lord, what a strange thing to say!" (*J'entre dans la vie. Derniers entretiens* [Paris: Cerf/Desclée De Brouwer, 1973] 140–41).

20. See nos. 117–19.

21. P. Maury, "La Vierge Marie dans le catholicisme contemporain," *Bulletin Fac. Théol. Prot.* (Paris, 1946) 6.

22. K. Barth, "Quatre études bibliques," *Foi et Vie*, nos. 85–86 (1936) 487.

23. S. de Diétrich, "Rôle de la Vierge Marie," *Cahiers d'Orgemont*, no. 58 (1966) 27.

24. A. and F. Dumas, *Marie de Nazareth* (Geneva: Labor et Fides, 1989) 98–99.

25. Luther, sermon in the year 1522; see *Kirchenpostille* (WA 10/1/1).

26. While Calvin refuses to call Mary "treasurer of grace" in the sense given to the term in the medieval tradition (see no. 282), he nonetheless reinterprets its meaning in accordance with the Reformation position: "In another sense, the Virgin is indeed a treasurer of grace. For she safeguarded the doctrine that opens the kingdom of heaven to us today and leads us to our Lord Jesus Christ; she safeguarded it as a deposit, and then through her we received it and are today built up by it. See, then, the honor God bestowed on her; see how we should think of her: not to stop short at her nor to turn her into an idol, but in order that by means of her we may be led to our Lord Jesus Christ, for that is precisely where she sends us" (25th Sermon of the *Gospel Harmony*, cited in *La Revue réformée*, no. 31 [1957/4] 37).

27. A. Piepkorn, "Mary's Place Within the People of God," *Marian Studies* 18 (1967) 82. [I did not have access to this periodical and have had to back-translate the passage from the French version. –Tr.].

28. See no. 298.

29. See nos. 214–27.

30. See the title of Ch. Drelincourt's work in no. 83.

Index of Biblical Citations (references are to numbered paragraphs of text)

OLD TESTAMENT

NEW TESTAMENT